OXFORD
UNIVERSITY PRESS

OXFORD
UNIVERSITY PRESS

Great Clarendon Street, Oxford, OX2 6DP, United Kingdom

Oxford University Press is a department of the University of Oxford. It furthers the University's objective of excellence in research, scholarship, and education by publishing worldwide. Oxford is a registered trade mark of Oxford University Press in the UK and in certain other countries

British Library Cataloguing in Publication Data

Data available

ISBN 978-019-841407-0

10 9 8 7 6 5 4 3 2 1

Printed in Great Britain by Bell and Bain Ltd., Glasgow

Acknowledgements

The publisher and author would like to thank the following for permission to use photographs and other copyright material:

Cover: Brownie Harris/Getty Images; **p3, 6-7:** Brownie Harris/Getty Images; **p10:** Christian Bertrand/Shutterstock; **p11(l):** abimages/Shutterstock; **p11(ml):** hurricanehank/Shutterstock; **p11(mr):** Michael D. Reid/Picfair; **p11(r):** Steve Preston; **p11(b):** Shutterstock; **p12:** Anthony Harvey/Getty Images; **p14:** Sophia Evans/The Guardian; **p13:** Sophia Evans/The Guardian; **p16:** Michael Loccisano/Getty Images; **p17:** Nnamdi Chiamogu; **p19:** AfriPics.com/Alamy Stock Photo; **p21:** Shutterstock; **p22:** Manor Photography/Alamy Stock Photo; **p25:** amc/Alamy Stock Photo; **p27:** Shutterstock; **p28:** lev radin/Shutterstock; **p29:** Adrian Brooks/Alamy Stock Photo; **p31:** Mary Evans Picture Library; **p37:** Peter Macdiarmid/Getty Images; **p41, 42:** Shutterstock; **p45:** Illustration © Lo Cole 2017/The Guardian; **p47:** Art Directors & TRIP/Alamy Stock Photo; **p50(l):** Brooks Kraft/Getty Images; **p50(m):** Evolution Design/Itay Sikolski; **p50(lr):** Evolution Design/Itay Sikolski; **p51:** Shutterstock; **p52:** Granger Historical Picture Archive/Alamy Stock Photo; **p53,55:** Shutterstock; **p58(t):** Russell Collins/Alamy Stock Photo; **p58(tr):** Featureflash Photo Agency/Shutterstock; **p58(tl):** Barrie Neil/Alamy Stock Photo; **p58(bl):** Dave J Hogan/Getty Images; **p58(br):** Everett Collection Inc/Alamy Stock Photo; **p59:** iStockphoto; **p60-61:** Shutterstock; **p62:** FALKENSTEINFOTO/Alamy Stock Photo; **p65:** Northfoto/Shutterstock; **p66:** dpa picture alliance/Alamy Stock Photo; **p69(t):** Courtesy of WWF; **p69(mt):** Courtesy of UNHCR; **p69(mb):** Courtesy of RSPCA; **p69(b):** Courtesy of OXFAM; **p70:** WENN Ltd/Alamy Stock Photo; **p72:** Glasshouse Images/Alamy Stock Photo; **p73:** Robert Beck/Getty Images; **p77:** The Essex Serpent by Sarah Perry is published by Serpent's Tail; **p78-79:** Trevor Batchelor/Picfair; **p81-90:** Shutterstock; **p92, p95:** F. S. Lincoln/Getty Images; **p97:** Shutterstock; **p98:** foodfolio/Alamy Stock Photo; **p100:** Glasshouse Images/Alamy Stock Photo; **p102(l):** Shutterstock; **p102(r):** View Pictures Ltd/Superstock; **p104:** Shutterstock; **p108:** Phil Wills/Alamy Stock Photo; **p110:** GARY DOAK/Alamy Stock Photo; **p114:** Janine Wiedel Photolibrary/Alamy Stock Photo; **p115:** Ilya Gridneff/AP/REX/Shutterstock; **p118:** Shutterstock; **p120:** ASHRAF SHAZLY/Getty Images; **p121:** ISSOUF SANOGO/Getty Images; **p126-132:** Shutterstock; **p133:** Justin Williams/REX/Shutterstock; **p135:** Shutterstock; **p143:** ALF DUJMOVITS/National Geographic Creative; **p144:** Art Directors & TRIP/Alamy Stock Photo; **p146, 147:** Shutterstock; **p148:** The Print Collector/Alamy Stock Photo; **p150:** Peter Etchells/Shutterstock; **p152-153:** Shutterstock; **p158:** Mountain climbers, c.1890-1900 (b/w photo), American Photographer, (19th century) / Private Collection / Avant-Demain / Bridgeman Images; **p160-161:** Chris Craggs/Alamy Stock Photo; **p164, 175:** Shutterstock; **p168:** Granger Historical Picture Archive/Alamy Stock Photo; **p169:** Chronicle/Alamy Stock Photo; **p170:** Terry Fincher. Photo Int/Alamy Stock Photo; **p171:** Hangman's noose in window frame, Mann, Robert (20th century) / Private Collection / © Special Photographers Archive / Bridgeman Images; **p177:** Chronicle/Alamy Stock Photo; **p180:** Shutterstock; **p182:** Jonathan Goldberg/Alamy Stock Photo; **p184:** Jeff Morgan 09/Alamy Stock Photo; **p185:** Image Source/Alamy Stock Photo; **p186:** Matthew Taylor/Alamy Stock Photo; **p187:** Shutterstock; **p188:** REX/Shutterstock; **p189:** dominika zarzycka/Shutterstock; **p192:** Shutterstock; **p195:** Enigma/Alamy Stock Photo; **p198:** Meibion/Alamy Stock Photo; **p203:** iStockphoto.

Every effort has been made to contact copyright holders of material reproduced in this book. Any omissions will be rectified in subsequent printings if notice is given to the publisher.

The author and publisher are grateful for permission to reprint the following copyright material:

Extract from Hansard, a Parliamentary publication, is Parliamentary © copyright and licensed under the Open Parliament Licence v3.0

Anonymous: 'What I'm Really Thinking: the supermarket delivery driver', *The Guardian*, 31 Jan 2015, copyright © Guardian News & Media Ltd 2015, 2017, reprinted by permission of GNM.

Chimamanda Ngozi Adichie: extracts from *Americanah* (Fourth Estate, 2014), copyright © Chimamanda Ngozi Adichie 2013, reprinted by permission of HarperCollins Publishers Ltd.

The Captive Animals' Protection Society: extract from 'Sad Eyes Empty Lives' (2011), www.captiveanimals.org, reprinted by permission of CAPS.

John Cheever: 'Reunion' from *Collected Stories* (Vintage, 2010), copyright © John Cheever 1979, reprinted by permission of The Random House Group Ltd and The Wylie Agency (UK) Ltd. All rights reserved.

Kathryn Chisholm: Letter to *Daily Mail*, 20 Jan 2016, reprinted by permission of Kate E Chisholm, Skerne Park Academy.

Daphne du Maurier: extracts from 'The Apple Tree', copyright © The Chichester Partnership 1938, from *The Birds and Other Stories* (Virago, 2004), reprinted by permission of Curtis Brown Group Ltd, London on behalf of The Chichester Partnership.

Martin Evans: 'Teenager who hacked governments worldwide is spared jail', *The Telegraph*, 20 July 2016, copyright © Telegraph Media Group Ltd 2016, reprinted by permission of TMG.

Neil Gaiman: extract from 'So many ways to die in Syria now. Neil Gaiman visits a refugee camp in Jordan', *The Guardian*, 21 May 2014, copyright © Guardian News & Media Ltd 2014, 2017, reprinted by permission of GNM.

Graham Greene: extracts from 'The Fallen Idol' first published as 'The Basement Room', copyright © Graham Greene 1935, from *The Third Man and The Fallen Idol* (Vintage Classics, 2001), reprinted by permission of David Higham Associates.

India Knight: 'Do loosen up, Miss - it's perfectly fine to be a jimjam mum' *The Times*, 31 Jan 2016, copyright © India Knight/ News Syndication 2016, reprinted by permission of News Syndication News UK & Ireland Ltd.

Felicity Lawrence: extract from 'These welfare reforms use hunger as a spur to work', *The Guardian*, 30 Jan 2012, copyright © Guardian News & Media Ltd. 2012, 2017, reprinted by permission of GNM

Lana Montgomery: 'A letter to…My daughter, who hates me for not being vegan', *The Guardian*, 4 Mar 2017, copyright © Guardian News & Media Ltd 2017, reprinted by permission of GNM

Grayson Perry (with Wendy Jones): extract from *Grayson Perry: Portrait of the Artist as a Young Girl* (Chatto & Windus, 2006), copyright © Wendy Jones and Grayson Perry 2006, reprinted by permission of The Random House Group Ltd.

Sarah Perry: extract from *The Essex Serpent* (Serpent's Tail, 2016), reprinted by permission of the publishers, Profile Books.

Albert Pierrepoint: extracts from *Executioner Pierrepoint: An Autobiography* (Eric Dobby, 2005) copyright © Albert Pierrepoint 1974, reprinted by permission of the heirs of Albert Pierrepoint and Eric Dobby Publishing Ltd.

Philip Pullman: 'Leave the Libraries alone; You don't understand their value', published on *False Economy*, www. falseeconomy.org.uk in 2011, reprinted by permission of United Agents LLP on behalf of Philip Pullman

Jay Rayner: extract from 'Shotgun: Restaurant review', *The Guardian*, 1 Nov 2015, copyright © Guardian News & Media Ltd 2015, 2017, reprinted by permission of GNM

Jo Randle: 'The day I made a difference: a radio ad helped me open my home to youngsters facing homelessness', *The Guardian*, 5 March 2017, copyright © Guardian News & Media Ltd 2017, reprinted by permission of GNM

Fay Weldon: extract from 'Weekend' from *Watching Me Watching You* (Hodder & Stoughton, 1981), copyright © Fay Weldon 1981, reprinted by permission of the author c/o Georgina Capel Associates Ltd, 29 Wardour Street, London W1D 6PS.

Jeanette Winterson: extract from 'Dark Christmas', in *Christmas Days: 12 stories and 12 feasts for 12 days* (Jonathan Cape, 2016), copyright © Jeanette Winterson 2016, reprinted by permission of The Random House Group Ltd.

Levison Wood: extracts from *Walking the Nile* (Simon & Schuster, 2014), copyright © Levison Wood 2014, reprinted by permission of Simon & Schuster UK.

Simon Worrall: 'Why K2 brings out the best and the worst in those who climb it', *National Geographic*, 13 Dec 2015, reprinted by permission of Abner Stein for the author.

Although we have made every effort to trace and contact all copyright holders before publication this has not been possible in all cases. If notified, the publisher will rectify any errors or omissions at the earliest opportunity.

CONTENTS

Preparing for the exam

AQA GCSE English Language specification overview

The exam papers

The grade you receive at the end of your AQA GCSE English Language course is entirely based on your performance in two exam papers. The following provides a summary of these two exam papers:

Exam paper	Reading and Writing questions and marks	Assessment Objectives	Timing	Marks (and % of GCSE)
Paper 1: Explorations in Creative Reading and Writing	**Section A: Reading** Exam text: • One unseen literature fiction text Exam questions and marks: • One short form question (1 x 4 marks) • Two longer form questions (2 x 8 marks) • One extended question (1 x 20 marks)	Reading: • AO1 • AO2 • AO4	1 hour 45 minutes	Reading: 40 marks (25% of GCSE) Writing: 40 marks (25% of GCSE) Paper 1 total: 80 marks (50% of GCSE)
	Section B: Writing Descriptive or narrative writing Exam question and marks: • One extended writing question (24 marks for content, 16 marks for technical accuracy)	Writing: • AO5 • AO6		
Paper 2: Writers' Viewpoints and Perspectives	**Section A: Reading** Exam texts: • One unseen non-fiction text and one unseen literary non-fiction text Exam questions and marks: • One short form question (1 x 4 marks) • Two longer form questions (1 x 8 marks and 1 x 12 marks) • One extended question (1 x 16 marks)	Reading: • AO1 • AO2 • AO3	1 hour 45 minutes	Reading: 40 marks (25% of GCSE) Writing: 40 marks (25% of GCSE) Paper 2 total: 80 marks (50% of GCSE)
	Section B: Writing Writing to present a viewpoint Exam question and marks: • One extended writing question (24 marks for content, 16 marks for technical accuracy)	Writing: • AO5 • AO6		

The Assessment Objectives (AOs)

Assessment Objectives are the skills that underpin all qualifications. Your GCSE English Language exam papers are testing six Assessment Objectives – AOs 1-6, whilst your Spoken Language tests AOs 7-9.

The following table outlines the Assessment Objectives for GCSE English Language and the exam paper questions where each Assessment Objective is tested:

Assessment Objective (AO)		Paper 1	Paper 2
AO1	• Identify and interpret explicit and implicit information and ideas	Question 1	Question 1 Question 2
	• Select and synthesize evidence from different texts	-	Question 2
AO2	Explain, comment on and analyse how writers use language and structure to achieve effects and influence readers, using relevant subject terminology to support their views	Question 2 Question 3	Question 3
AO3	Compare writers' ideas and perspectives, as well as how these are conveyed, across two or more texts	-	Question 4
AO4	Evaluate texts critically and support this with appropriate textual references	Question 4	-
AO5	Communicate clearly, effectively and imaginatively, selecting and adapting tone, style and register for different forms, purposes and audiences. Organize information and ideas, using structural and grammatical features to support coherence and cohesion of texts	Question 5	Question 5
AO6	Candidates must use a range of vocabulary and sentence structures for clarity, purpose and effect, with accurate spelling and punctuation.	Question 5	Question 5
AO7	Demonstrate presentation skills in a formal setting	n/a	n/a
AO8	Listen and respond appropriately to spoken language, including to questions and feedback on presentations	n/a	n/a
AO9	Use spoken Standard English effectively in speeches and presentations.	n/a	n/a

What sorts of texts and stimulus tasks will the exam papers include?

Paper 1

Section A: Reading will include the following types of text:

- A prose literature text from either the 20th or 21st century
- It will be an extract from a novel or short story.
- It will focus on openings, endings, narrative perspectives and points of view, narrative or descriptive passages, character, atmospheric descriptions and other appropriate narrative and descriptive approaches.

Section B: Writing will include the following stimulus:

- There will be a choice of scenario, either a written prompt or a visual image related to the topic of the reading text in Section A. The scenario sets out a context for writing with a set audience, purpose and form that will differ from those specified in Paper 2.
- You will produce your own writing, inspired by the topic that you responded to in Section A.

Paper 2

Section A: Reading will include the following types of text:

- Two linked sources (one non-fiction and one literary non-fiction) from different time periods (one 19th century and one from either the 20th or 21st century. The sources will also be from different genres so you need to think about how each presents a perspective or viewpoint to influence the reader.

Section B: Writing will include the following stimulus:

- You will produce a written text for a specified audience, purpose and form in which you give your own perspective on the theme that has been introduced in Section A.

Spoken Language

As well as preparing for the two GCSE English Language exams, your course also includes Spoken Language assessment. This is **not** an exam. Instead your tutor sets and marks the assessments.

There are three separate Assessment Objectives covering Spoken Language – AO7, AO8 and AO9. At the end of your course you will receive a separate endorsement for Spoken Language, which means it will not count towards your final 9-1 grade.

Introduction to this book

How this book will help you

Develop your reading and writing skills

The primary aim of this book is to develop and improve your reading and writing skills. Crucially however, in this book, you will be doing this in the context of what the exam papers will be asking of you at the end of your course. So, the skills you will be practising throughout this book are ideal preparation for your two English Language exam papers.

Explore the types of texts that you will face in the exams

In your English Language exams you will have to respond to a number of unseen texts. In order to prepare you fully for the range and types of text that you might face in the exam, Chapters 1 and 2 of this book are structured thematically so you can explore the connections between texts. This is ideal preparation for your exams as the unseen texts in your exam papers will be of different types (fiction and non-fiction), from different historical periods (from the 19th, 20th and 21st centuries) and will in some instances be connected.

Become familiar with the Assessment Objectives and exam paper requirements

Assessment Objectives are the skills that underpin all GCSEs. Your GCSE English Language exam papers are testing six Assessment Objectives (see pages 4 and 5). Chapters 1 to 2 of this book explore a selection of texts thematically so that you can practise and develop your reading and writing skills in the context of the Assessment Objectives. Chapters 3 to 6 focus on the Reading and Writing sections of Paper 1 and Paper 2. The Reading chapters guide you through each of the Reading examination questions whilst the Writing chapters explore all the key skills you need to demonstrate in the writing tasks in the two exams.

Monitor progress through assessments

This book includes end of chapter assessments and sample exam-style questions that enable you to demonstrate what you have learnt and help your tutor assess your progress. Each of these assessments will prepare you for the types of task that you will be facing in your GCSE English Language exams. The sample papers at the end of the book give you the opportunity to bring together all that you have been learning and practising in a 'mock' exam situation.

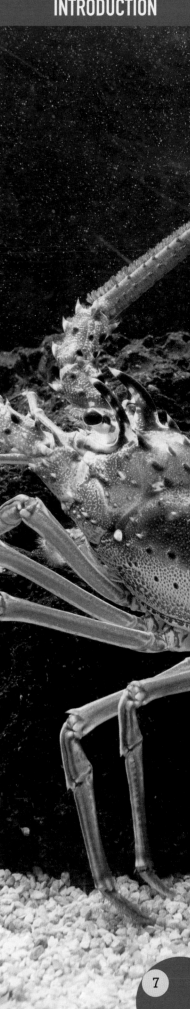

How is the book structured?

Chapters 1 to 2

Chapters 1 to 2 of this book take a thematic approach to developing your reading and writing skills, addressing the same Assessment Objectives. This revisiting of Assessment Objectives and supported practising of tasks, in different thematic contexts and with different texts, will ensure that your skills improve.

Chapter 3 to 6

Chapters 3 to 6 then pull together the skills that you have been practising and look closely at each of the questions in the two exam papers. This section of the book outlines the key skills to demonstrate to pass your exams. This will help prepare you for 'mock' exam papers at the end of the book.

What are the main features within this book?

Activities

To develop your reading responses to the wide range of texts included in this book as well as developing your writing skills, you will find activities all linked to the types of question you will face in your exams. The source texts reflect the types of text that you will face in your two exams.

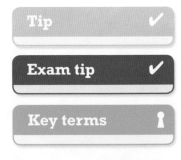

Tips, Key terms and glossed words

These features help support your understanding of key terms, concepts and more difficult words within a source text. These therefore enable you to concentrate fully on developing your exam response skills.

Progress check

In addition to the summative end of chapter assessments, you will also find regular formative assessments in the form of 'Progress checks'. These enable you to decide how confident you feel about your English skills.

A note on spelling

Certain words, for example 'synthesize' and 'organize', have been spelt with 'ize' throughout this book. It is equally acceptable to spell these words and others with 'ise'.

Further GCSE English Language and English Literature student resources

AQA GCSE English Language and English Literature Kerboodle: Resources and Assessment

What is Kerboodle?

Kerboodle is a brand new online subscription-based platform provided by Oxford University Press.

Kerboodle: Resources and Assessment

This AQA GCSE English Language and English Literature Kerboodle: Resources and Assessment provides support and resources to enable English departments and individual teachers to plan their GCSE courses and deliver effective, personalized lessons. Resources include:

- Teaching and learning materials, including:
  - A bank of assignable spelling, punctuation and grammar interactive activities to improve technical accuracy
  - Revision features for language and literature, including exam tip videos with Peter Ellison and Peter Buckroyd
- Assessment resources, including:
  - Marked sample answers and mark schemes
  - Editable versions of the end-of-chapter Student Book assessments and sample exam papers
- Professional development materials, including:
  - Seven specially-commissioned film-based CPD units devised by Geoff Barton, with classroom lesson footage, additional interviews and supporting written resources
  - A SPAG guide for GCSE teaching

AQA GCSE English Language Revision Workbook Targeting Grade 5 and Targeting Grades 6 to 9

These write-in workbooks, structured around the individual exam questions, help students achieve grades 5 to 9 by taking active control of their revision. Ideal for use in school or at home, the workbooks:

- guide students through the exam papers and the individual questions
- provide extensive practice opportunities, revision tips and specification guidance
- engage and motivate through the full colour design and targeted support
- feature self-evaluation checklists and regular formative assessment opportunities
- include sample responses and full sample exam papers.

1 Changing tastes

From *Come Dine with Me* to Raymond Blanc; from high street fashion to Vivienne Westwood, choices for 21st-century Western consumers are endless.

Were you the sort of child who was a fussy eater... and have you become a young adult who is willing to try anything? Are you particular about where you buy your clothes and what you will wear? Has that changed as you have grown older?

Fashion tastes in food, clothes, art and music continue to change, and sometimes even return to where they started, as 'retro' becomes the new 'now'.

In this chapter you will consider different attitudes to changing tastes, by reading a range of writing from different genres and times.

Skills and Assessment Objectives

All the reading and writing skills in this chapter are linked to the Assessment Objectives (AOs) which will be tested in your GCSE English Language exams.

Reading skills include how to:

- find and interpret information and ideas
- find and synthesize evidence from texts to support your views
- explain how writers use language for particular effects
- examine how writers organize texts for particular effects

- compare writers' ideas and attitudes
- make judgements about how a writer makes a piece of writing effective.

Writing skills include how to:

- write imaginatively in different forms for particular purposes and readers
- organize your written ideas in a carefully crafted way
- use accurate grammar, spelling and punctuation.

Activity 1

a. Look at each image below linked to food, art or fashion. Decide how you would rate them in terms of your personal taste. Choose from 1 to 5, with 5 being the most positive rating.

1

2

3

4

5

b. With a partner, discuss the images and their position in terms of 21st-century taste. Are there any that you really like? Are there any that you hate? What are your reasons and what are the key factors that affect others' perceptions of them?

You might like to consider:

- how a person's taste for these elements is influenced by age, race, gender, or where they live
- differences in tastes you have seen if you have travelled abroad
- your changing tastes as you have grown up.

1 Food

Skills and objectives

- To find and interpret information and ideas (AO1)
- To analyse how the writer uses language and structure to entertain and persuade his readers (AO2)

Key term

review: a text that gives opinion and information about a commodity such as a book, film or meal, and makes a judgement about it

Some journalists get paid for eating out and then writing about it. Here, the food critic Jay Rayner comments on the style and menu of a new South American restaurant in London that he has visited for this purpose. Read the opening to his **review**.

Shotgun: restaurant review

Shotgun, 26 Kingly Street, London W1 (020 3137 7252). Meal for two, including drinks and service: £80

In the modern age of flash and bravura, every new restaurant must have its Instagrammable dish. And here it comes at Shotgun. It's listed as pig's ear and sour pancakes, and that's exactly what it is: a whole pig's ear, complete with the mechanics for joining it to the skull,
5   alongside soft lacy folded pancakes, like antimacassars[1] that have been tidied away. The ear is so anatomically[2] intact that it looks like the plate has been genetically modified to listen into your conversation.

If so, it would hear my companion muttering 'the horror, the horror' followed by the grating roll of her eyeballs in their sockets at the
10 shameless display of culinary machismo. She is, I think, missing a trick. The ear has been long and slow cooked to something close to a jelly, then dressed with a sweet sour sauce, and heavily sprinkled with crushed peanuts and sliced spring onions. You slice off a piece, wrap it in a frond of pancake, and settle into a glorious interplay of
15 gelatinous and crunchy, of salt and sweet.

[1]antimacassar – a piece of cloth put over the back of a chair for decoration or protection

[2]anatomically – scientifically accurate with regard to the structure of the body

The information and ideas contained in this article are both **explicit** and **implicit**. A review text relies on a balance between factual information to inform the reader, and persuasion and opinion to reflect the writer's point of view.

Activity 1

a. Look at the title and first paragraph of the article. One explicit piece of information is the name of the restaurant: 'Shotgun'.

Find four other explicit pieces of information from the list below. Choose the most straightforward facts that no one can argue with.

- A meal for two including drinks and service costs £80 at Shotgun.
- The restaurant is in London.
- The reviewer is repulsed by the unusual dish on the menu.
- The reviewer's companion has an eye illness.
- Pig's ear and sweet pancakes is on the menu.
- The pancakes are folded.
- It looks like the plate has its own listening ears.
- The dish is pig's ear jelly.

b. The second paragraph contains both explicit and implicit information on Rayner's views about the restaurant and its dishes.

Use the sentence starters below to write three points about Rayner's views in paragraph 2, using evidence from the text to support your points.

- Rayner thinks that...
- He also suggests that...
- His words imply that he feels...

The food critic uses a range of language and structural features to entertain his readers and persuade them towards his opinion.

The **structure** of an extract is how the writer has built a text or paragraph. It considers the relationship between the beginning, middle and end and whether or not there are shifts and changes marked by different sections of a text.

Look again at the second paragraph of the text, reproduced below. Notice how the writer has structured the paragraph into three sections with a shift in the middle.

> **Key terms** 🔑
>
> **structure:** how a text is built and organized in sections
>
> **contrast:** strong difference

Section 1

Section 2

Section 3

If so, it would hear my companion muttering 'the horror, the horror' followed by the grating roll of her eyeballs in their sockets at the shameless display of culinary machismo. She is, I think, missing a trick. The ear has been long and slow cooked to something close to a jelly, then dressed with a sweet sour sauce, and heavily sprinkled with crushed peanuts and sliced spring onions. You slice off a piece, wrap it in a frond of pancake, and settle into a glorious interplay of gelatinous and crunchy, of salt and sweet.

Activity 2

a. Identify the focus of the second and third sections by completing the sentences below. The first section has been completed as an example for you:

- The first section of paragraph 2 focuses on... *the reviewer's dinner companion.*
- The second section of paragraph 2 focuses on...
- The third section of paragraph 2 focuses on...

b. Pinpoint where the shift in focus occurs in this paragraph.

c. The writer structures this paragraph in three sections to emphasize a **contrast**. What two ideas is he contrasting in this paragraph?

Remember the specialist terminology that you already know for analysing the English language. Language features include:

- devices that you know from studying literature texts, such as figurative language, alliteration, imagery and descriptive language

- words with specific grammatical functions such as nouns or **verbs**

- rhetorical devices such as repetition, familiar references, exaggeration (hyperbole) and sets of three.

Key term

verbs: words that mark actions, events, processes and states. They usually have a tense, either present, past or future.

Activity 3

a. Read the review on page 12. As you read, think about this question: how does the writer use language to convey his opinions about the food?

b. Look at the answer at the bottom of this page to see how one student has responded to this question. Notice how the first paragraph is structured by 'PEE'.

Point: Making a point

Evidence: Selecting evidence

Explanation: Explaining its effect, in relation to the question.

c. Complete the other three paragraphs in the student answer below. Each paragraph should focus on one language feature, and use the PEE structure.

d. Add a final paragraph of your own, identifying another relevant language feature.

e. Once you have finished writing, check your work and identify the PEE in each paragraph, either by annotation, or underlining each in a different colour.

How does the writer use language to convey his opinions about the food?

Firstly, he uses up-to-date terminology linked to social media to convey how fascinating the look of the dish is. He refers to the 'Instagrammable dish' which suggests that the meal is fascinating and worth taking a photo of. — Point / Evidence / Explanation

In addition, he uses a simile to describe the pancakes' appearance to engage the reader in what the dish looks like...

He humorously exaggerates the disgusted reaction of his companion to the dish. For example,...

He uses verbs to describe the skills of cooking and the pleasure of eating. This can be seen in the phrase...

2 Fashion

Skills and objectives

- To select and synthesize evidence from two extracts (AO1)
- To evaluate how effectively the writer creates setting and character (AO4)

Key terms

setting: the place or surroundings where an event takes place or something is positioned

dialogue: direct speech

actions: the things someone does

The Nigerian writer Chimamanda Ngozi Adichie uses her characters to consider a range of issues she feels strongly about. In her novel *Americanah*, she considers the different settings, cultures and fashions of modern Nigeria and modern America. She uses the **setting**, **dialogue** and **actions** of the characters of her novel to focus on her personal and political concerns. In this novel, the topic of how black women style their hair is considered as a political issue. Some black women feel pressured to straighten their naturally curly hair to look more European. In the extracts you will read in this section, the main character wears her hair braided.

Read an early section of the novel which introduces the setting and the main character Ifemelu who has come to America from Nigeria. She has just begun a successful career in a top American university in Princeton.

Extract A from *Americanah* by Chimamanda Ngozi Adichie

Princeton, in the summer, smelled of nothing, and although Ifemelu liked the tranquil greenness of the many trees, the clean streets and stately homes, the delicately overpriced shops, and the quiet, abiding air of earned grace, it was this, the lack of a smell, that most appealed
5 to her, perhaps because the other American cities she knew well had all smelled distinctly. Philadelphia had the musty scent of history. New Haven smelled of neglect. Baltimore smelled of brine, and Brooklyn of sun-warmed garbage. But Princeton had no smell. She liked taking deep breaths here. She liked watching the locals who drove with
10 pointed courtesy and parked their latest-model cars outside the organic grocery store on Nassau Street or outside the sushi restaurants or outside the ice cream shop that had fifty different flavours including red pepper or outside the post office where effusive staff bounded out to greet them at the entrance. She liked the campus, grave with
15 knowledge, the Gothic buildings with their vine-laced walls, and the way everything transformed, in the half-light of night, into a ghostly scene. She liked, most of all, that in this place of affluent ease, she could pretend to be someone else, someone specially admitted into a hallowed American club, someone adorned with certainty.

20 But she did not like that she had to go to Trenton to braid her hair. It was unreasonable to expect a braiding salon in Princeton—the few black locals she had seen were so light-skinned and lank-haired she could not imagine them wearing braids—and yet as she waited at Princeton Junction station for the train, on an afternoon ablaze with heat, she wondered why there *was* no place where she could braid her hair.

Activity 1

The writer conveys a range of facts about Princeton, as well as Ifemelu's opinions, that help the reader learn about her character and values.

a. Which of the following statements about Princeton does this extract state are true?

1 It has trees.

2 It has a wide range of restaurants.

3 It has a university.

4 It has a range of shops.

5 It does not smell of garbage.

6 It does not have a braiding salon.

7 There are many Nigerians living there.

Key term

infer: work out meaning from what someone implies rather than from an explicit statement

b. Now look at the statements below taken from the passage. The writer chooses to list certain details. From these, the reader can **infer** Ifemelu's attitude to Princeton.

Ifemelu liked:

1 'the tranquil greenness of the many trees'

2 'the clean streets and stately homes'

3 'the delicately overpriced shops'

4 'the quiet, abiding air of earned grace'

From what you have learned in these quotations, decide on a phrase that best summarizes Ifemelu's attitude to Princeton.

c. Then complete the following sentence:

> The writer conveys Ifemelu's attitude to Princeton as...

d. Select two more quotations from lines 1–19 that support your phrase. Then write a PEE paragraph using these quotations to explain Ifemelu's attitude to Princeton.

e. The structural shift in the second paragraph reveals that Ifemelu is unable to find a braiding salon for black women in Princeton.

With a partner, discuss the following question:

> What does this detail about the lack of the salon add to our understanding of Ifemelu's character and her attitudes?

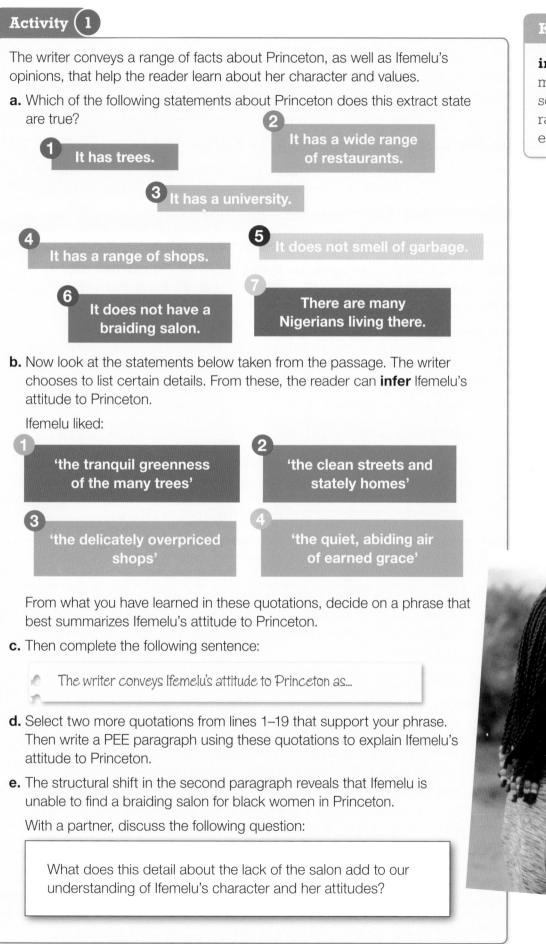

As the story develops, the writer reveals more information about Ifemelu to interest the reader. A new setting and characters are introduced in her visit to a braiding salon in Trenton. These help the reader understand more about Ifemelu's attitudes. The writer considers the experience of moving from Nigeria to America and how this can affect people.

Extract B from *Americanah* by Chimamanda Ngozi Adichie

'Here we are!' he said, parking in front of a shabby block. The salon was in the middle, between a Chinese restaurant called Happy Joy and a convenience store that sold lottery tickets. Inside, the room was thick with disregard*, the paint peeling, the walls plastered with large posters of braided hairstyles and smaller posters that said QUICK TAX

5 REFUND. Three women, all in T-shirts and knee-length shorts, were working on the hair of seated customers. A small TV mounted on a corner of the wall, the volume a little too loud, was showing a Nigerian film: a man beating his wife, the wife cowering and shouting, the poor audio quality jarring.

'Hi!' Ifemelu said.

10 They all turned to look at her, but only one, who had to be the eponymous Mariama, said, 'Hi. Welcome.'

'I'd like to get braids.'

'What kind of braids you want?'

Ifemelu said she wanted a medium kinky twist and asked how much it was.

15 'Two hundred,' Mariama said.

'I paid one sixty last month.' She had last braided her hair three months ago.

Mariama said nothing for a while, her eyes back on the hair she was braiding.

'So one sixty?' Ifemelu asked.

Mariama shrugged and smiled. 'Okay, but you have to come back next time. Sit down.
20 Wait for Aisha. She will finish soon.' Mariama pointed at the smallest of the braiders, who had a skin condition, pinkish-cream whorls of discoloration on her arms and neck that looked worryingly infectious.

'Hi, Aisha,' Ifemelu said.

Aisha glanced at Ifemelu, nodding ever so slightly, her face blank, almost forbidding in its
25 expressionlessness. There was something strange about her.

Ifemelu sat close to the door; the fan on the chipped table was turned on high but did little for the stuffiness in the room. Next to the fan were combs, packets of hair attachments, magazines bulky with loose pages, piles of colourful DVDs. A broom was propped in one corner, near the candy dispenser and the rusty hair dryer that had not
30 been used in a hundred years. On the TV screen, a father was beating two children, wooden punches that hit the air above their heads.

'No! Bad father! Bad man!' the other braider said, staring at the TV and flinching.

'You from Nigeria?' Mariama asked.

'Yes,' Ifemelu said. 'Where are you from?'

35 'Me and my sister Halima are from Mali. Aisha is from Senegal,' Mariama said.

Aisha did not look up, but Halima smiled at Ifemelu, a smile that, in its warm knowingness, said welcome to a fellow African; she would not smile at an American in the same way. She was severely cross-eyed, pupils darting in opposite directions, so that Ifemelu felt thrown off-balance, not sure which of Halima's eyes was on her.

40 Ifemelu fanned herself with a magazine. 'It's so hot,' she said. At least, these women would not say to her, 'You're hot? But you're from Africa!'

'This heat wave is very bad. Sorry the air conditioner broke yesterday,' Mariama said.

Ifemelu knew the air conditioner had not broken yesterday, it had been broken for much longer, perhaps it had always been broken; still she nodded and said that perhaps it had 45 packed up from overuse. The phone rang. Mariama picked it up and after a minute said, 'Come now,' the very words that had made Ifemelu stop making appointments with African hair braiding salons. 'Come now,' they always said, and then you arrived to find two people waiting to get micro braids and still the owner would tell you, 'Wait, my sister is coming to help.' The phone rang again and Mariama spoke in French, her voice rising, 50 and she stopped braiding to gesture with her hand as she shouted into the phone. Then she unfolded a yellow Western Union form from her pocket and began reading out the numbers. 'Trois! Cinq! Non, non, cinq!'

The woman whose hair she was braiding in tiny, painful-looking cornrows said sharply, 'Come on! I'm not spending the whole day here!'

55 'Sorry, sorry,' Mariama said. Still, she finished repeating the Western Union numbers before she continued braiding, the phone lodged between her shoulder and ear.

*disregard – the state of paying no attention to something

Key terms

adjective: a word that describes something named by a noun or pronoun

adjectival phrase: a group of words that explain a noun or pronoun; it can come before or after the noun/pronoun

Activity 2

In Extract B, the writer shifts to a contrasting setting from Ifemelu's viewpoint. She includes details that show the difference between African and American cultures. She shows Ifemelu's attitude towards African ways, now she has been successful in America.

a. Read through Extract B and select five quotations that establish this setting and its inhabitants as very different from Princeton. Include factual information, plus what you can infer from Ifemelu's observations. You might consider:

- the place
- how characters are described
- how characters act
- what characters say.

b. Copy and complete the table below, to compare Ifemelu's perceptions of the different places described in Extracts A and B. An example is completed for you.

Use quotations to support your answers. As you select these:

- notice how the writer uses language, particularly **adjectives** and **adjectival phrases**, to help the reader picture each setting
- notice how the writer uses the structural device of contrast between Extracts A and B to help us understand Ifemelu's attitudes and experiences.

	Extract A	Extract B
The appearance of the buildings	Expensive and well-kept 'stately homes' 'Gothic buildings with their vine-laced walls'	Run down and more deprived 'a shabby block'
The shops		
Money		
People's manners		
People's values		
Your idea here...		
Your idea here...		

c. When you have completed the table, underline any adjectives or adjectival phrases included in your quotations.

d. Compare your answers with a partner's. With your partner, discuss these questions:

- How does the author use the structural device of contrast to help us understand Ifemelu's character and experiences?

- Why do you think Ifemelu is irritated by some of what she finds in the salon? Does the author suggest Ifemelu likes anything about the salon? Find evidence in the text to support your opinions.

3 Appearance matters

- To communicate imaginatively, focusing in particular on creating character and setting (AO5)
- To write clearly and accurately (AO6)

In the extracts you read from *Americanah*, you examined how a skilled writer used setting, character, dialogue and structure to engage her reader.

In this unit, you are going to look at the sample exam questions below.

Either: Write a short story about an event suggested by the picture below.

Or: Write the opening description of a story which begins with the phrase, 'It's a well known fact that appearance matters.'

You do not need to take the text or picture literally: 'suggested by' means you can use them as a starting point.

A story can be based on real experience since we often write more effectively about something we know. You do not need to write a detailed, action-packed story; a well-written account focusing on an incident or small event can be more powerful than attempting to address a subject of huge scope.

Stage 1: Ideas generation

Before you start planning, you should think of some ideas that will:

- be interesting for an adult reader (remember, adults may find the perspective of a young person interesting to read about)
- be possible to write in 40 minutes, including planning time
- present you with a setting and a character or two (which could include yourself as 'I')
- present some minor conflict/contrast and resolution – for example, a problem or an issue that can be rounded off with an ending.

Tip ✓

Don't try to include a large range of characters and events (like in an action film) in a short piece of writing as there may not be time to do them justice.

Activity 1

a. Look at the rough ideas of another student below. Which would you rule out and why? Discuss your ideas in pairs and then as a class.

b. Decide on the best two ideas and give reasons for your answer. Use the questions below to help you with your choices.

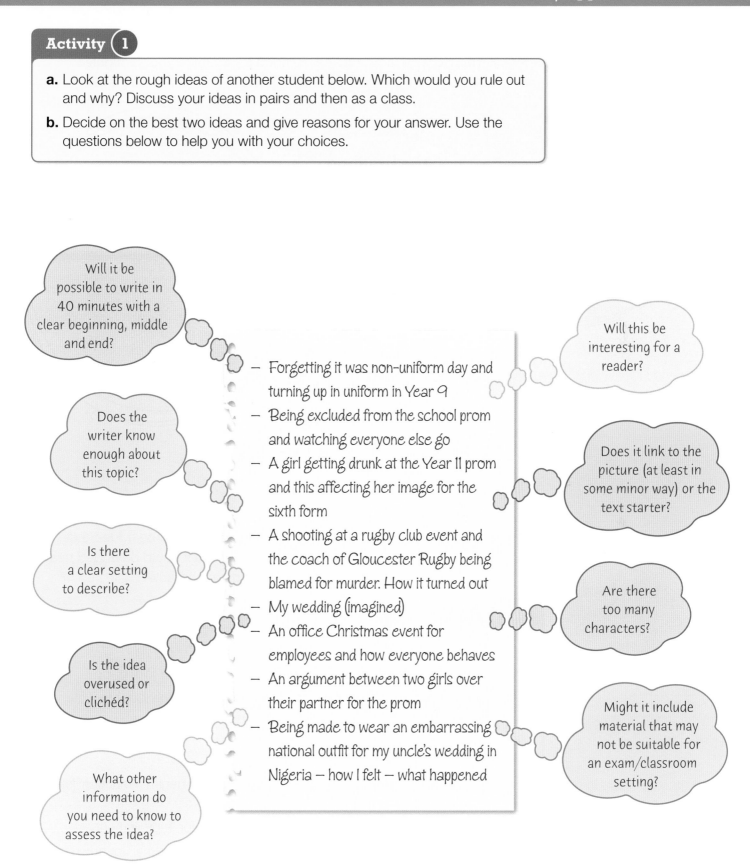

Will it be possible to write in 40 minutes with a clear beginning, middle and end?

Does the writer know enough about this topic?

Is there a clear setting to describe?

Is the idea overused or clichéd?

What other information do you need to know to assess the idea?

Will this be interesting for a reader?

Does it link to the picture (at least in some minor way) or the text starter?

Are there too many characters?

Might it include material that may not be suitable for an exam/classroom setting?

— Forgetting it was non-uniform day and turning up in uniform in Year 9

— Being excluded from the school prom and watching everyone else go

— A girl getting drunk at the Year 11 prom and this affecting her image for the sixth form

— A shooting at a rugby club event and the coach of Gloucester Rugby being blamed for murder. How it turned out

— My wedding (imagined)

— An office Christmas event for employees and how everyone behaves

— An argument between two girls over their partner for the prom

— Being made to wear an embarrassing national outfit for my uncle's wedding in Nigeria – how I felt – what happened

Planning

Before starting to write a narrative, you need to organize your thoughts. Look at the notes below based on Extract B from *Americanah* on pages 18–19.

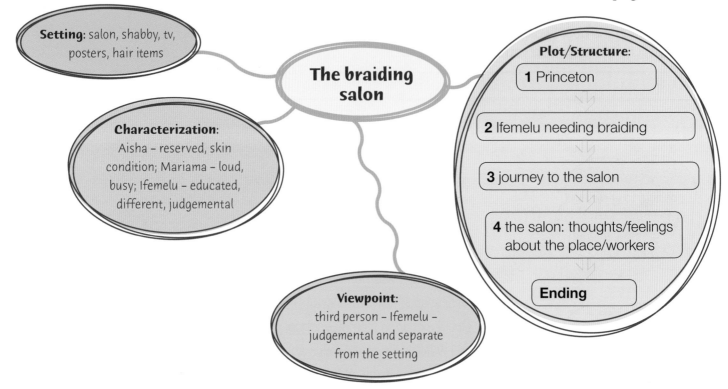

Remember that your reading of *Americanah* was only an extract from a larger novel. But to complete the plan above, a final incident could be added that finishes it as a short piece. Can you think of a way that it could be ended neatly, with some kind of change or realization by the main character?

Activity 2

a. Complete a similar plan for your own description of an incident.

- **setting:** Where and when will your incident/description take place?
- **characterization:** Who is the incident about/who is the focus for your description?
- **viewpoint:** Who is telling the incident? You or a first-person narrator (using I) or a third-person narrator (using he/she)
- **plot/structure:** How will your description/incident begin? What conflict will be encountered and how will it be resolved?

b. Discuss your notes with a partner, adding any ideas for improvement.

c. Decide how much direct speech you want to use in your story. Jot down some ideas to try out your characters' voices. Dialogue should not make up more than a quarter of your story. Look back at the *Americanah* extracts and notice how much is used in each one.

Creating character

Activity 3

a. With a partner, discuss the differences between the two paragraphs written by students below. How does the use of detail included by the writer help to create different impressions of Ben? Which is more engaging and why?

Georgia

I looked across at Ben. He was so smart in his Armani suit and I felt jealous because he was always given everything. Everyone always admired him and he always had so much money but I knew he was not a good person. He just wanted to be noticed and to get importance from what he owned. His parents always bought him whatever he wanted, from clothes and shoes even to a brand new car for his 18th. Everything he did and said annoyed me.

Helen

I looked across at Ben and he looked back at me, with a slight sneer on his face. 'Nice suit mate,' he smirked, throwing a look at Callum who moved closer to him as though they were a team in their dark Armani suits. He slid his car keys casually across the table to the group of girls. 'Keep them in your bag will you, Ella?' he demanded, as he lounged back in his chair, stretching his long legs in front of him. I took a deep breath to calm my nerves.

b. Decide how you want the reader to react to a character (or yourself if you are writing autobiographically) and make a note of some details about them that will achieve this effect.

- Choose two physical features to mention that might suggest something about their personality.

- Choose two actions that might reveal something about your character's personality.

Creating setting and atmosphere

Activity 4

a. With a partner, discuss the differences between two students' paragraphs below. How do the details included by the writer help to create two very different atmospheres?

Sarah

It was early evening, the air was warm and the fast paced music in the car made my heart beat faster at what was to come. My hair was pristine, my dress perfect and I was ready for my entrance. As we pulled up to the venue, the lights outside sparkled as we would. We had finally made it...

Colin

It was early evening and the drone of the radio chewed over the problems of the world news. I looked down at my shoes – slightly scuffed at the ends, and in keeping with the sweet wrappers and old parking tickets of the last year which littered the vehicle. The rain beat steadily outside, tapping relentlessly like fingers on a desk. It would be a long night.

b. Decide how you want the reader to feel throughout your story and make a note of some details that will achieve this through the setting of your writing. You can use this to reflect the mood of your characters as well as to help your reader picture the scene.

Stage 2: Writing

Activity 5

Using all the work you have done so far, write a response to the following task:

> Your favourite magazine is running a creative writing competition.
> Write an imaginative short story suggested by the picture below.
>
>
>
> Aim to write a short, structured piece of six to eight paragraphs with a clear sense of beginning and end.

Stage 3: Proofreading

Activity 6

a. When you have finished your short story, you need to proofread your work. Complete the checklist below for accuracy:

- paragraphing ☐
- a range of different sentence types ☐
- capital letters used only for proper nouns, beginning of sentences and start of direct speech ☐
- spelling – use a dictionary when necessary ☐
- examples of interesting vocabulary. ☐

  Beware of including too much direct speech. Some conversation is fine, but it should not make up the majority of your story.

b. Read your work aloud to check that it all makes sense and is punctuated correctly. Make any changes to improve your work.

c. Read your first paragraph to your partner. Will it 'hook' your reader? Make any changes needed.

Tip ✓ SPAG

Paragraphing

A new paragraph is needed to mark a change of:

- topic
- time
- place
- speaker (when using direct speech).

4 The freedom of choice

- To select and synthesize evidence from different texts (AO1)
- To examine how a writer uses language and structure for particular effects (AO2)
- To compare writers' ideas and perspectives (AO3)
- To proofread and edit writing (AO6)

Fashion has been a source of concern in our society for centuries. As the texts in this section show, clothing is linked to power; the people that shape or control fashion have power over those who wear it.

Anchoring a reading text

Writers craft their texts by choosing words carefully to influence their readers. There are various checks you must do with an unseen text, before you can evaluate the skills of a writer.

When reading an unseen text for the first time, check if you have been given the following information:

- when it was written
- who it was written by – are you told anything about their background?
- where it was published.

In this way you can find clues about the writer's intention and the effects intended. For any new text you must establish:

> **P**urpose – is it to persuade, describe, explain, instruct, inform, entertain, or argue, or a combination of these?
>
> **A**udience – is it for a specific person or is it for a wider readership? Is the reader young, old, male or female, or is it for the general public?
>
> **T**ext type – is it a letter, newspaper article, magazine article, review, **obituary** or speech?

You cannot assess how effective a writer's language choices are unless you have established the original intention.

Key term

obituary: a news article reporting the recent death of a person, usually includes details about their life and achievements

Exam tip ✔

Remember, in exam conditions, use **PAT** for an unseen text before you begin annotating it and writing your answer.

Establishing the writer's viewpoint

Judging others on the basis of their clothes is a common feature of modern society. In January 2016, a primary school headteacher wrote to parents asking them not to wear their pyjamas when taking their children to school. Now read an article from *The Times* about this event by the outspoken journalist India Knight.

Do loosen up, Miss — it's perfectly fine to be a jimjam mum

by India Knight

A primary school head in Darlington last week asked parents to dress appropriately for the school run. Kate Chisholm wrote: 'I have noticed there has been an increasing tendency
5 for parents to escort children to and from school while still wearing their pyjamas and, on occasion, even slippers. Could I please ask that when you are escorting your children, you take the time to dress appropriately in daywear
10 that is suitable for the weather conditions?'

She said that some parents wore pyjamas and slippers to school assemblies and meetings, though I'm guessing they were 9am rather than 6pm events. 'If we're to raise standards,
15 it's not too much to ask parents to have a wash and get dressed,' she said sternly.

Chisholm is right, of course, even if telling people how to dress is not in her remit. And yet, as someone who spent years going to school in
20 cosy pyjamas with a coat on top and Ugg boots on my feet, my heart is on the side of the useless parents, who I'm sure are perfectly clean, by the way. (The wearing of pyjamas does not preclude washing your face and cleaning your teeth.)

25 When my older children were little, there was a period when I was dropping one off at nursery and coming back to spend the day with the baby. I didn't see the point of getting up 20 minutes earlier in order to stick on a frock
30 in readiness for a morning of tidying, laundry, messy play and even messier eating. Also, I was really tired. When you're permanently

longing for a nap, the wearing of pyjamas gives you hope: should the merest opportunity arise, you're good to go.   35

When my sons were both at school, I found the time I could spend getting dressed was better spent cooking them a hot breakfast, rather than laying out nutritionally useless cereal and doing my lipstick.   40

There's an emotional element at play, too. The women — I never saw pyjamaed men — have young children and stay at home (the women who work are dressed for the office).

The fact is, women define themselves   45
sartorially[1]. For me, no longer needing to have

an office wardrobe was a source of delight. Tight things with buttons and buckles, stiff fabrics, collars — clothes that needed ironing 50 every morning — were a thing of the past.

If those clothes symbolized work, then pyjamas — more specifically pyjama bottoms with a baggy jumper on top — symbolized cosy domesticity. (I should add that for a minority 55 of women pyjamas are a sign of not coping. Ordering them to get dressed isn't very helpful.)

I'd like to tell you I grew out of this — it was 20 years ago — but that wouldn't entirely be true, as my daughter would attest. I never went 60 back to work in an office, and my strong dislike of workwear never went away. I don't wear

daytime pyjamas any more, but if I'm spending the day at home working, I don't entirely get dressed 'properly' either.

The trick is finding an outfit that is soft and 65 cosy yet vaguely flattering, and that wouldn't cause you to die of shame if your accountant dropped in. Some people think that you work better when you're properly dressed, but I would feel absurd sitting at my laptop with 70 heels and a blow-dry.

Clothes maketh the woman, and if the woman is comfortable rather than trussed up[2] as she goes about her day — well, I call that a small triumph. 75

---

[1]sartorially – related to clothes or style of dress

[2]trussed up – tied up uncomfortably to prevent escape

Tip ✓

Use line references to help you refer to specific quotations. You will need to work out the line numbers in between those numbers marked. Line references can be useful when writing about structure.

Activity 1

Before you analyse the language of a text, you must establish the Purpose, Audience and Text type of the source. Copy and complete a table like this one on the texts you have read so far.

Source Text	Purpose	Audience	Text type
Text 1: 'Shotgun' (page 12)			
Text 2: *Americanah* (pages 16–19)			
Text 3: 'Do loosen up, Miss...' (pages 29–30)			

Activity 2

a. Can you identify India Knight's viewpoint as expressed in this article? Use the sentence starter below to begin your statement:

> In this article, Knight expresses her viewpoint that...

b. Summarize the full content of the article. Your challenge is to use only four clear sentences to structure your summary.

c. Compare your paragraph with a partner's. Check that you have included the key issues and evidence. Have you both written using complete, grammatically-correct sentences?

d. Make any necessary changes to your paragraph.

Now read the text below from American newspaper *The Lily* written by women for women in the 19th century. *The Lily* argued for a woman's right to wear practical clothing such as men's trousers. At this time, women wore uncomfortable clothes such as corsets and long dresses. The article takes this argument further by suggesting that there is no reason why men *or* women should be ridiculed by wearing a style of clothing that is usually worn by the opposite gender.

Male Bloomers

The Lily newspaper, 1854

Many of our brother editors are aiming their wit and ridicule at those gentlemen who have donned the Shawl[1] as a comfortable article of wearing apparel in cold weather.

5 There is a class of men who seem to think it their especial business to superintend[2] the wardrobes of both men and women, and if any dare to depart from their ideas of propriety[3], they forthwith launch out into all sorts of witticisms 10 and hard names, and proclaim their opinions, their likes and dislikes, with all the importance of authorized dictators. As to the Shawl, it would be well if it could be banished from use entirely; as it is an inconvenient and injurious article of apparel, 15 owing to its requiring both hands to keep it on, and thereby tending to contract the chest, and cause stooping shoulders.

But if worn at all, men have the same right to it that women have. If they find it comfortable, 20 that is enough; and no one has a right to object to their wearing it because women wear shawls. The sack coats[4] of the men, and the sacks of the women at the present time are cut very nearly after the same pattern. Both 25 find them comfortable and convenient, without being burdensome. The hands are left free to swing at the sides, or use at pleasure. This is the most comfortable and useful garment for the street, for both men and women, ever introduced; — and must either dispense with[5] 30 this comfortable garment because it is worn by the other?

In our opinion people have a right to wear about what they please — what may suit their own wants, or their fancy; and while we claim 35 the right to decide for ourself in our own case, we accord the largest liberty to our brothers and sisters in the same matter. Let each one study to please himself and herself, and – let other people mind their own business. 40

[1]Shawl – a large piece of material like a scarf draped over the shoulders and upper body

[2]superintend – oversee, be in charge of

[3]propriety – what is regarded as proper or decent

[4]sack coat – a loose-fitting coat hanging straight down from the shoulders, particularly as worn by men in the 19th and early 20th centuries

[5]dispense with – get rid of

Some 19th-century texts can be challenging to understand. You need to:

- read the text through more than once
- use the clues given to you by the introductory text
- use the glossary which will explain unfamiliar words.

Activity 3

a. Read 'Male Bloomers' on page 31. Select four points below that correctly reflect the writer's arguments.

- The police have been checking men's wardrobes.
- Some men have been criticizing other men's clothes.
- Upper-class men do not like working-class men's clothing.
- Women do not like men wearing women's clothes.
- The shawl is an annoying piece of clothing to wear.
- Men have a right to wear shawls.
- Men have been wearing their wives' shawls.
- The sack coat is a practical item of clothing.
- Women should be allowed to wear coats that are similar to men's.
- Men used to wear shawls in the past so they could return to doing that.

b. Find the shortest quotation possible that supports each of your selected points well.

c. Add two more sentences, using your own words, which summarize the two final points made by the writer in the last paragraph.

Key terms

tone: a way of writing which conveys the writer's attitude towards either the reader or the subject matter

synthesize: to combine information and ideas from different texts

Activity 4

The writer of 'Male Bloomers' is using a variety of language devices to convey a logical and persuasive argument.

a. Can you identify any of the language features below in the passage? Find evidence for at least six of the points below and copy out a precise quotation to support it.

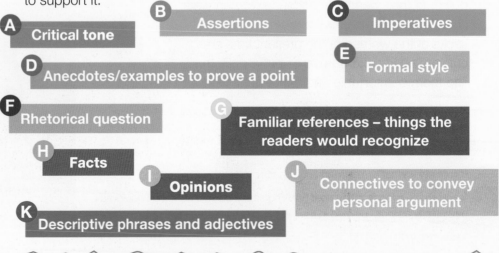

A Critical tone

B Assertions

C Imperatives

D Anecdotes/examples to prove a point

E Formal style

F Rhetorical question

G Familiar references – things the readers would recognize

H Facts

I Opinions

J Connectives to convey personal argument

K Descriptive phrases and adjectives

b. Now answer the question below by developing your points into PEE points.

> In this article the writer argues her viewpoint that men and women should be able to wear the same style clothing if they choose to. Explain how the writer uses language to persuade her readers of this viewpoint.

Here is an example of how one student developed their response to Activity 4:

The writer uses adjectives to praise certain items of clothing to show why both men and women should be able to wear them. For example she describes sack coats as 'comfortable and convenient'. She gives reasons for her argument such as the practicality and the comfort of these garments. The alliteration of the 'c' sound in this phrase emphasizes how logical her argument is that everyone would like wearing them.

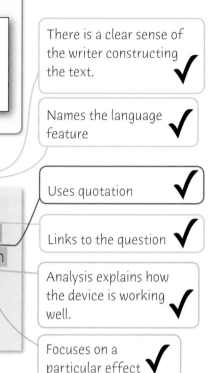

There is a clear sense of the writer constructing the text. ✔

Names the language feature ✔

Uses quotation ✔

Links to the question ✔

Analysis explains how the device is working well. ✔

Focuses on a particular effect ✔

Synthesizing evidence

Both 'Do loosen up, Miss' and 'Male Bloomers' are articles which deal with the subject of society's judgements about clothing, but they are written in different centuries and from different perspectives. You are going to select and **synthesize** evidence from the two texts.

Activity 5

Re-read 'Do loosen up, Miss' by India Knight on pages 29–30.

a. With a partner, identify whether the writer uses any of the same language devices that you noticed in 'Male Bloomers'. Can you identify any other language devices? Look carefully at the terms given in Activity 4 to help you.

b. Now consider the way Knight divides the text by using different focuses.

- Identify the lines where the writer uses methods A–D below. You can then see how the writer has built up her argument.
- Are any of them used more than once?
- Write out the order in which she uses these techniques, using the letters below:

A Statement(s) of personal opinion

B Factual example/True story

C Personal example/anecdote

D Resulting point(s) of argument

c. Discuss with a partner why Knight might have chosen to combine these methods in her text and how they complement each other.

Activity 6

Compare the two writers' attitudes to clothing and society in 'Do loosen up, Miss' and 'Male Bloomers'.

Complete a table like the one below to plan your comparison.

- Add one more point about the writer's attitude in column 1.
- Add a short quotation or a line reference to relevant evidence in columns 2 and 3.
- Explain the point you are making beneath the quotation.

One row has been completed for you as an example.

Writer's attitude	'Do loosen up, Miss'	'Male Bloomers'
Dislikes society making judgements about what is acceptable	'not in her remit' (line 18).	'There is a class of…' (line 5).
	'remit' emphasizes that this headteacher is interfering in personal life	sarcastic, scornful tone
Thinks that views about clothing are particularly harsh on women		
Thinks that practicality is the most important aspect of dress		
Your idea here...		

Tip ✓

When you compare two texts, use one paragraph for each point of comparison, using column 1 of your plan to establish the overall point. Write about both texts in that paragraph so that you really are comparing or contrasting information about two pieces of writing.

Activity 7

a. Using both sources and the plan you completed in Activity 6, write a full answer to the following question. Use PEE to make sure that each of your points include evidence and analysis of the writer's techniques.

Remember to write out the question first and underline the key words.

> Compare how the two writers convey their different attitudes to society's judgements about clothing in 'Do loosen up, Miss' and 'Male Bloomers'.

In your answer you should:

- compare their different attitudes
- compare the methods they use to convey their attitudes
- support your ideas with quotations from both texts.

b. Proofread your work. Try reading it aloud to check for careless errors.

Progress check

In this chapter you have developed some key skills. Complete the progress check below to see how confident you now feel about applying these skills.

a. Re-read your answer to Activity 7 and check you have satisfied each of the skills below.

Key Skills I can:	Confident I can do this.	OK Sometimes I can do this.	Not sure I need to practise this more.
find and interpret information and ideas			
find and synthesize evidence from the text to support my views			
analyse how the writer uses language to achieve particular effects			
analyse how the writer uses structure to achieve particular effects			
compare writers' ideas and perspectives			
communicate imaginatively, in particular creating character and setting in narrative writing			
plan and organize my ideas so that my writing is clear and accurate			
proofread and edit my writing			

b. If your answer is missing any of these skills, or you think they could be stronger, go back to your answer and make changes. You could work with a partner to offer each other feedback on your responses.

Assessment

This section tests all the reading and writing skills that you have learned in this chapter.

Read the extract below and complete the activities that follow. The extract is from a modern newspaper article that suggests that government cuts in benefits are a return to 18th-century views, when politicians believed that hunger would push the poor into working hard.

These welfare changes use hunger as a spur to work

by Felicity Lawrence

The coalition government's welfare reforms and its attack on wages cast poverty in Britain in 18th-century terms.

5 The daily experience of hunger is reappearing in Britain, one of the world's richest countries. Behind the undoubtedly good private work to relieve it is a public moral failure.

The H&F foodbank is located in one of
10 those streets that have become enclaves of stratospheric[1] City wealth in the last three decades. They are intensely relaxed about being filthy rich here – Chelsea tractors[2] on parade outside £2m–£3m 19th-century
15 red-brick villas, home cinemas displayed in immaculate architectural extensions of sheet glass. Next door to the foodbank is the Hurlingham clinic, where the elite's need for expensive physical perfection can be met
20 with 'aesthetic procedures' from injectable fillers to cellulite management.

[…] Daphine Aikens, H&F foodbank's manager, ran through the reasons her visitors find themselves unable to eat: 22% are on incomes so low, in work or on benefits, that
25 the smallest upset tips them into crisis; 10% have had their benefits reassessed and can no longer make ends meet; 8% have fallen into debt, often as a result of soaring energy bills, or transport costs; 7% are recently
30 unemployed and delays in benefit claims have left them temporarily destitute.

[…] One afternoon last week, I watched the parcels go out. Audrey, shedding tears of shame, had given most of her pension
35 cheque to her daughter and grandchildren following a fire that destroyed their home. The daughter, a single parent and pharmacist – retraining as a teacher so she could look after the children in the holidays – had not
40 been able to afford insurance, so had been left with nothing. Audrey was having the grandchildren for the weekend but had no money to feed them. She had been living on a diet of breakfast cereal and crackers with
45 small bits of cheese.

João, from Portugal, had been fully employed in low-paid catering jobs since 2004 but was made redundant this year. He fell into debt because he was not allowed to escape his mobile phone contract. He had applied for the two vacancies at the job centre that morning, but they had gone. He had been going two to three days at a time without food, going to bed to conserve energy. How could hunger spur him to greater efforts to work when there are no jobs?

A pregnant mother with two children and no food for their supper, husband at work, too distressed to talk; a young man with mental health problems, moved from a hostel to a flat and waiting for his benefits to be transferred, no food for nearly three days and no money for heating ... the litany[3] of hardship is humbling. The archaic[4] attitude that this sort of hunger is individual failure rather than the experience of victims of circumstance, or often of a capricious[5] economic system beyond their control, was abandoned well over a century ago. Let's not go back to it now.

[1]stratospheric – extreme

[2]Chelsea tractors – any expensive 4x4 driven in a city environment as a status symbol (informal/slang)

[3]litany – repetitive series or list

[4]archaic – old-fashioned

[5]capricious – changeable

This activity will secure your knowledge about how to **identify and interpret information (AO1).**

Activity 1

a. Look at lines 9–21 of the article. Write four factual statements about the area where the foodbank is located.

b. Look at lines 33–46 which contain both explicit and implicit ideas. Write one sentence that summarizes what is implied about Audrey.

Exam tip ✔

Remember to refer to the writer of fiction or non-fiction articles by their surname. This is a convention of formal writing.

Tip

- A simple sentence can be used to emphasize a simple statement and give clear information
- A minor sentence can be used to draw attention to a single idea or emotion
- A compound sentence can be used to give extra detail or link two ideas together
- A complex sentence can show relationships between clauses, such as contrast, cause and effect, contrast and time relationships

This activity will secure your knowledge about **how writers use text structure and sentence forms to create effects (AO2).**

Activity 2

a. Read the features listed below used by the writer to structure her writing. Link them to the relevant paragraph of the article 'These welfare changes...' Some features may be used more than once. Some paragraphs may link to more than one feature:

- conclusion
- setting
- real-life story/example
- introduction
- factual information about foodbank users
- writer's viewpoint.

b. Identify an example of each type of sentence used by the writer: simple, minor, compound and complex. Explain their effect on the reader, using a table like the one below.

Sentence	Sentence type	Explanation of effect
'The daily experience of hunger is reappearing in Britain.'	Simple	The writer uses a clear simple sentence to establish the focus of her article.

This activity will remind you **how writers use language to create effects for the reader (AO2).**

Activity 3

a. The writer uses the words 'filthy' and 'Chelsea tractors' in the second paragraph. What does her choice of language tell us about her views on the people who live near the foodbank?

b. In the final paragraph what do the phrases 'victims of circumstance' and 'beyond their control' suggest about the writer's views on the foodbank users?

Now read the extract below from a letter written by the famous author Oscar Wilde in 1897. He himself was imprisoned as a result of being a gay man. This letter was written after his release. Wilde complains about the dismissal of a prison warden who gave extra food to children in his prison.

Sir,—

I learn with great regret, through an extract from the columns of your paper, that the warder Martin, of Reading Prison, has been dismissed by the Prison Commissioners for having given some sweet biscuits to a little hungry child. I saw the three children myself on the Monday

5 preceding my release. [...] They were quite small children, the youngest—the one to whom the warder gave the biscuits—being a tiny little chap, for whom they had evidently been unable to find clothes small enough to fit. I had, of course, seen many children in prison during the two years during which I was myself confined. Wandsworth Prison, especially, contained always a large number of children. But the little child I saw on the afternoon of Monday, the 17th, at

10 Reading, was tinier than any one of them. I need not say how utterly distressed I was to see these children at Reading, for I knew the treatment in store for them. The cruelty that is practised by day and night on children in English prisons is incredible, except to those who have witnessed it and are aware of the brutality of the system.

The second thing from which a child suffers in prison is hunger. The food that is given to it

15 consists of a piece of usually badly-baked prison bread and a tin of water for breakfast at half-past seven. At twelve o'clock it gets dinner, composed of a tin of coarse Indian meal stirabout[1], and at half-past five it gets a piece of dry bread and a tin of water for its supper. This diet in the case of a strong grown man is always productive of illness of some kind, chiefly of course diarrhœa, with its attendant weakness. In fact in a big prison astringent[2] medicines are served out regularly

20 by the warders as a matter of course. In the case of a child, the child is, as a rule, incapable of eating the food at all. Anyone who knows anything about children knows how easily a child's digestion is upset by a fit of crying, or trouble and mental distress of any kind. A child who has been crying all day long, and perhaps half the night, in a lonely dimly-lit cell, and is preyed upon by terror, simply cannot eat food of this coarse, horrible kind. In the case of the little child to

25 whom Warder Martin gave the biscuits, the child was crying with hunger on Tuesday morning, and utterly unable to eat the bread and water served to it for its breakfast. Martin went out after the breakfasts had been served and bought the few sweet biscuits for the child rather than see it starving. It was a beautiful action on his part, and was so recognized by the child, who, utterly unconscious of the regulation of the Prison Board, told one of the senior warders how kind this

30 junior warder had been to him. The result was, of course, a report and a dismissal.

The case is a special instance of the cruelty inseparable from a stupid system, for the present Governor of Reading is a man of gentle and humane[3] character, greatly liked and respected by all the prisoners. He is very popular with the prisoners and with the warders. Indeed he has quite elevated[4] the whole tone of the prison-life. [...] Under his predecessor the system was carried out with the greatest harshness and stupidity.

[1]stirabout – porridge made by stirring oatmeal in boiling water or milk

[2]astringent – sharp, bitter

[3]humane – kind

[4]elevated – lifted, improved

In this activity you will **select and synthesize evidence from different texts (AO1).**

Activity 4

Look at the statements below which address the similarities identified in the lives of the vulnerable people in both texts on pages 36-37 and 39. Select brief quotations from each text to support the point made and explain them with a comment. The first example is done for you.

The victims in both texts are helped by others.
Wilde mentions 'the warder gave the biscuits' which shows him understanding that they are hungry. The 'Welfare Changes' text describes the work of charity foodbanks and refers to 'H&F foodbank's manager' which suggests that help is on a bigger scale and well-organized.

The victims in both texts are hungry.

The victims in both texts have restricted access to food in their lives.

The victims in both texts are poor.

Activity 5

a. Use the table below to compare the writers' viewpoints about vulnerable people and how society is treating them.

b. Add relevant quotations from the text to support your points. You could write the line reference in the table to help you.

Views expressed	Article: 'These welfare changes…'	Oscar Wilde letter
SIMILARITIES in viewpoint		
1. Concern that vulnerable people are going hungry	Adults are poor and can't buy food for themselves and family	Children are hungry – too upset to eat poor prison food
2. People in power are unreasonable and cause their suffering		
3. The people helping them deserve respect		
4.		
DIFFERENCES in viewpoint		
1.		
2.		

c. Decide whether the writer of each text has a sympathetic, negative or mixed viewpoint overall about the people they are writing about. Complete the sentences below:

> Overall the writer of the article 'These welfare changes' has a sympathetic/negative/mixed view about users of foodbanks. This is because...
>
> I think Oscar Wilde's letter has a sympathetic/negative/mixed view about the children. This is because...

d. Using the sentences you wrote above and your notes from the table, write a three-paragraph response to the following task:

> Compare the writers' views on foodbank users and imprisoned children. Use your own words but also quote from both texts to support what you say.

This activity will secure your knowledge of how to **evaluate writing using references to the text (AO4).**

Tip ✓

Remember that the question is asking you to consider the writers' views rather than just the factual differences between their topics.

Tip ✓

You might like to refer back to your previous work on pages 28–34 to look at similarities and differences, and use of the PEE structure to formulate your writing.

Activity 6

a. Look back at the two non-fiction texts in this section on pages 36-39. Decide which one you think is most successful at engaging the reader. Think carefully about the effects that the writer has created using language and structure.

b. Explain which text is the more successful as an information text and choose two quotations from that text as evidence for your opinion.

This activity will secure your knowledge of how to **write an imaginative story, using clear, accurate English (AO5, AO6).**

Activity 7

SPAG

Write a short narrative story suggested by this photograph. Remember to:

- plan the plot (what happens)

- think about characters – their appearance and personality

- consider setting – how you will convey atmosphere

- make your opening interest the reader

- organize your writing in paragraphs

- proofread your work, checking spelling, punctuation and grammar.

2 Work, money and success

> 'Try not to become a man of success. Rather become a man of value.'
>
> Albert Einstein, physicist (1879–1955)

Many people link their own sense of self and success to their job and their income. Modern success is often linked to money, power, status and even fame. They are slippery things to gain, and even more difficult to hold on to.

Yet for others, success is linked to entirely different things, for example: family, interests, morality, religion, a social life or a balanced combination of those things. Some people manage to connect their interests and work so strongly that their pleasure has become their way of life and even the way to fund that life.

In this chapter you will read various definitions of success, as well as considering the choices famous *and* ordinary people have made about work and money in their lives.

Skills and Assessment Objectives

All the reading and writing skills in this chapter are linked to the Assessment Objectives (AOs) which will be tested in your GCSE English Language exams.

Reading skills include how to:

- identify and interpret explicit and implicit ideas
- select and synthesize evidence from different texts
- analyse how writers use language and structure to achieve effects
- compare writers' ideas across different texts
- compare how writers convey their ideas
- evaluate how successful writers have been.

Writing skills include how to:

- write for different purposes
- communicate clearly
- choose the right tone and style for your writing
- organize your ideas and use structural features
- use a range of vocabulary for clarity, purpose and effect.

By the end of the chapter, you will have considered a range of perspectives on work, life and success and might even change your views as a result.

Activity 1

Think about your own ambitions and your own ideas about your future working life.

Consider your possible choices of employment once you leave education. Rate the elements below from 0–5 in terms of their importance to you in your choice of a job. (0 is 'no importance' and 5 is 'very important'.)

	1	2	3	4	5
Using your current talents or skills					
The possibility of training and learning new skills					
Intellectual stimulation					
Practical or physical elements					
Helping others					
Work-life balance					
Regular working hours in the daytime					
Clear career structure to 'work your way up'					
High salary					
Enough money to live on					
Security (e.g. paid holidays, a pension and a permanent work contract)					
Personal enjoyment					
Possibility of fame					
Increase of status or importance					
Working with like-minded people					
Social opportunities (e.g. lots of young people)					
Location (e.g. near your current home, or the opposite: somewhere abroad)					
Opportunity to travel					

Compare your ideas with a partner. Discuss two or three ideas you might be considering for your future working life and how you are going to achieve them.

1 On the road

The pace of life for many people in the western world has increased. Many adults are working more and need the convenience of longer opening hours, supermarket food and home deliveries. This has spawned a range of jobs that were not common in past generations.

Read the private thoughts below of one such worker who delivers supermarket groceries, published in *The Guardian* newspaper.

What I'm really thinking: the supermarket delivery driver

I've already been working for hours before I arrive at your house, having loaded my truck with the multiple orders
5 of crates of beer and mineral water, over 20kg a crate.

I'm hot, irritable, tired and probably hungry. I maintain my cheerful demeanour[1], though,
10 anxious to chat with you and show I am not the inarticulate[2] buffoon[3] you evidently suppose I am.

You insist on me bringing your
15 shopping deep into the bowels of your home, as opposed to dumping it on the doorstep. I accede[4], puffing through your ground floor in the inevitably
20 vain hope of a small tip to supplement my meagre, below-London-living-wage salary.

As you shut your Farrow & Ball[5] painted door, I slog on to my
25 next delivery (only 14 to go) at a 'media' company round the corner. I know I will be spoken to like an imbecile by a twenty-something bearded hipster, and
30 have to cart dozens of boxes of company-funded wine and beer through the maze of Apple Macs, pool tables and quirky, Lego-filled 'interaction spaces'
to the kitchen. 35

The delivery after that, though, will make it all worthwhile, as I will get to chat with the elderly disabled couple on the eighth floor of a tower block, who regale[6] me with 40 fascinating stories of their travels. They are always grateful of my trek up the urine-soaked stairwell, and when I leave, the lady will smilingly press a pound coin into 45 my hand and thank me. I get to forget my woes, the aches in my back and shoulders, the parking attendant hovering round my van and the 12 remaining deliveries 50 dotted all over the city, my faith in humanity and kindness restored.

[1]demeanour – manner

[2]inarticulate – not good at expressing ideas or feelings clearly

[3]buffoon – clown

[4]accede – agree

[5]Farrow & Ball – an expensive brand of paint

[6]regale – entertain

Using quotations

In the exam you must use quotations to support most points you make. Time is limited so select short, sharp quotations with the key words that prove your point. Don't waste time in copying out long extracts from the text. Try instead to build short quotations into your sentences. Look at this example of a quotation below and how you could use small parts of it to support a point.

Original quotation: 'The woman, despite the fact that she felt distressed and unwell, smiled at her customers.'

Exam point with embedded quotation: The woman is professional as she 'smiled at her customers' despite feeling unwell.

Exam point with quotation after a colon: The woman maintains a professional friendly appearance: she 'smiled at her customers'.

Activity 1

Read the facts below about the worker in the article opposite. Find the *shortest possible* quotations to support each point. Choose no more than five or six words to support the points you have been given.

A The driver tries to look happy.

B He has been working for some time before arriving at the first house.

C He has been lifting heavy loads.

D He is often asked to bring shopping into the house rather than delivering it to the doorstep.

E He does not feel physically comfortable.

Activity 2

The writer has structured his article in five paragraphs to focus on the different aspects of his experience as a delivery driver.

a. Look carefully at each paragraph and give a short title to each one to summarize its focus.

> **1** Arrival at the doorstep

> **2**

> **3**

> **4**

> **5**

b. Explain how the paragraph structure of the text helps the reader understand the delivery driver's work.

Use some of the phrases in the phrase bank below, as well as your own ideas, to support your writing about these.

Phrase bank:
- shift in time
- shift in place/setting
- contrast between two ideas
- shift in focus
- This helps the reader look at the job from a different perspective.
- This encourages the reader to understand how drivers are treated by customers.
- This introduces the idea of the pressure employers put on drivers.
- This emphasizes the contrast between his life and some of his customers.
- This encourages the reader to sympathize with the driver.

The delivery driver chooses language carefully to convey his attitudes to his job and customers. It creates a particular tone that helps the reader to understand his views.

Activity 3

a. Look at the quotations below and identify the tone of each one. You can use some of the suggestions below to help you or use your own ideas.

Quotations:

'You insist on me bringing your shopping deep into the bowels of your home'

'the inevitably vain hope of a small tip to supplement my meagre, below-London-living-wage salary'

'your Farrow & Ball painted door'

'the maze of Apple Macs, pool tables and quirky, Lego-filled "interaction spaces"'

'the lady will smilingly press a pound coin into my hand and thank me'

Examples of tone:

admiring   cutting   sarcastic   condescending

angry   miserable   resentful   depressed

critical   happy   contented   appreciative

b. Then explain what each quotation suggests about the writer's view of his customers.

c. The article on page 44 is a good example of how language and structure work together to convey the writer's intention. Look back at the order of the quotations above in the text, and think about the questions below:

- How does the tone develop as the writing is built up? Can you trace this build-up?

- How does the piece end?

- How does the ending contrast with the beginning?

- What does it reveal overall about the man's attitude towards his job?

Writing

When you write a response to the writing tasks in the exam, you will be assessed on how well you:

- communicate clearly, selecting and adapting tone, style and register for a specific purpose and audience (AO5)

- use a range of vocabulary for clarity, purpose and effect (AO6).

Activity 4

Use what you have learned about the language and structure of this text to write your own personal account entitled, 'What I'm really thinking'.

Remember the audience for your piece is both *The Guardian* newspaper readers and your teacher or lecturer. Your topics and language must take that audience into account.

Think about the various roles you might play in your work, home and social life: the student, the employee, the older sibling, the referee, the Saturday sales assistant, the grandchild. What could you list in relation to your own life?

Which of these might provide an engaging focus for a piece of personal writing revealing some of your thoughts, feelings and activities related to the role? You could use a real-life situation or enrich it with some imaginative elements.

Once you have decided on your focus, consider the following questions to plan your answer:

Tone:
- How do you feel about that role?
- Are you able to convey mixed feelings such as those in 'The supermarket delivery driver' article?

Structure:
- Are there different elements of that role that you could use to plan and structure a four-paragraph piece of writing?
- For example, 'The supermarket delivery driver' uses the idea of being 'on the road' to move between one delivery, the expectation of the next, and the memory of a regular customer.
- You might use time, place or people to structure your piece of writing.

Vocabulary:
- Is there particular vocabulary that you can use to engage your reader?
- Is there specialist vocabulary to do with that role, whether it has a sport, learning or work focus?
- Is there any language that is specific to age or area that you can use to convey a sense of voice in your writing?
- Beware of slipping into slang and grammatical errors without realizing.

Copy and complete the spider diagram below to jot down your thoughts and ideas in response to these questions.

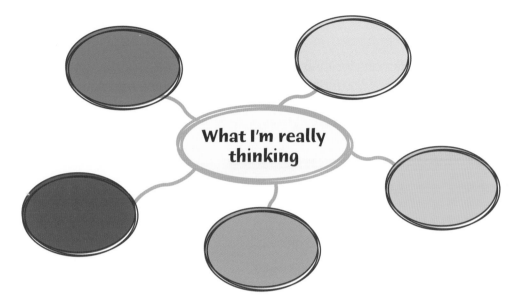

Then note down the topic of each paragraph, to plan the sequence of your writing. Use a flowchart, like the one below.

1

2

3

4

Then use your flowchart plan to write your article.

Proofreading

Activity 5

a. Proofread your writing to check for errors. Remember that your GCSE exam requires accuracy in spelling, punctuation and grammar.

b. Check to make sure that you have used varied, and some sophisticated vocabulary in your writing.

c. Underline five words or phrases you have used that show you have chosen vocabulary carefully to interest your reader. If you are not able to do this, replace these examples with more sophisticated vocabulary. You could use a thesaurus to help you find alternatives.

2 Workplace politics

Skills and objectives

- To identify and interpret explicit and implicit ideas (AO1)

- To analyse how writers use language and structure to achieve effects (AO2)

- To evaluate a text critically and support this with textual references (AO4)

One company famous for their workplaces is Google. Google is proud of its unusual workplaces around the world as settings which enable workers to do well in their tasks.

Activity 1

Spend a few minutes looking at the pictures of Google offices below, noticing every detail. With a partner, discuss the questions below. Make sure you have evidence to justify your views.

- What typical aspects of an office workplace are present?
- What do you notice that surprises you?
- What does the office layout suggest about the company and its values?

The text opposite is adapted from the short story 'Business and Ethics' published in 1915. It is about a business that makes dyes, such as those used for paints or material. 'Business and Ethics' focuses on the relationship between business and honesty. The author establishes the office setting and characters, to examine power in the workplace.

As you read the opening:

● note any unfamiliar words

● check the glossary for help with vocabulary

● read it once or twice until you are confident you could explain the events to another person in three or four sentences.

Extract A adapted from 'Business and Ethics'[1] by Redfield Ingalls

In the dingy office of A. Brown & Co., manufacturers of dyes, things were humming. Every clerk was bent over his desk, hard and cheerfully at work, and there was a general air of bustle and efficiency.

That was because A. Brown stood in the doorway of his private office looking on.

The portly[2] head of the firm watched the scene complacently[3] for a few minutes. Then, catching the eye
5 of his young but efficient private secretary, he beckoned him with an air of mystery to the inner sanctum[4].

The secretary, who was sharp of eye and alert of manner, rose at once and followed, though it was not the custom of A. Brown to summon him thus. His employer sank ponderously[5] into his swivel chair and motioned to the secretary to shut the door and take a seat. Then for a minute or so he was silent, playing with his massive gold watch chain and studying the young man through puckered[6] lids. But if
10 the secretary was perturbed he did not show it.

'Mr. Sloane,' began Brown, at length, in his heavy voice, 'you have been with the firm now how long — six or five months, ain't it?'

'Nearly six,' the dapper young man confirmed briskly.

'You're a smart feller, Mr. Sloane,' his employer continued, 'already you've picked up a lot about
15 dyeing. A fine dyer you should make. Now, Mr. Sloane, I'm going to fire you.'

The secretary's eyebrows went up a trifle, but otherwise he showed no great perturbation[7]. Perhaps a certain elephantine[8] playfulness in the big man's tone reassured him.

Brown went on, with a fat chuckle. 'I'm a business man, Mr. Sloane, first and last, and nobody don't never get one over on me.'

[1]ethics – moral principles, values of what is right and wrong

[2]portly – plump, large

[3]complacently – with satisfaction

[4]inner sanctum – private place where few people are allowed to go

[5]ponderously – thoughtfully and slowly

[6]puckered – wrinkled

[7]perturbation – concern, worry

[8]elephantine – like an elephant, large and awkward

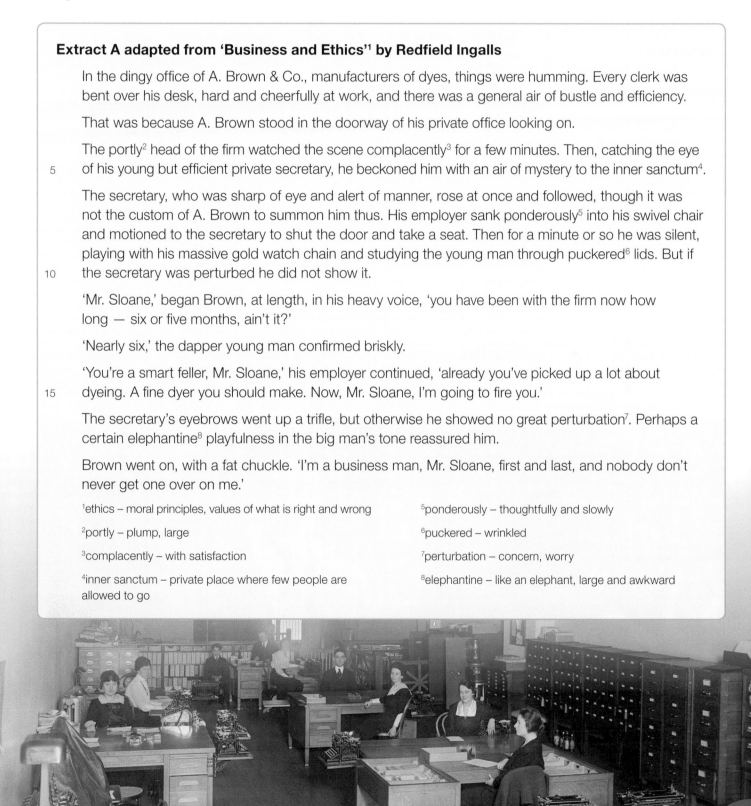

Writing about language

The writer uses language to convey the setting and atmosphere of an old-fashioned office and the character of the boss. He crafts his words to develop the **theme** of power in this opening.

When writing about language, you must explore how the writer's word choices affect the reader.

● You must identify the *specific effect* the writer achieves.

● The writer's choices are shaping the readers' thoughts and feelings about what is being portrayed.

Before you complete this activity, refresh your memory on grammatical terminology that is relevant to this passage:

common noun – identifies a person, place or thing, but does not need a capital letter

proper noun – identifies a unique person, place or thing and needs a capital letter

adjective – a word that describes something named by a noun or a pronoun

adjectival phrase – a phrase that describes something named by a noun or a pronoun

connective – a word that joins phrases or sentences, such as: 'moreover', 'as a result', 'furthermore', 'in addition', 'not only' etc.

Activity 2

One of the language features in this passage is the writer's use of description. Read the quotations below and consider their effect on the reader.

'things were humming'

'The portly head of the firm watched the scene complacently'

'he was silent, playing with his massive gold watch chain and studying the young man through puckered lids'

'sharp of eye and alert of manner'

'it was not the custom of A. Brown to summon him thus'

'young but efficient private secretary'

'in the dingy office'

'nobody don't never get one over on me'

Now answer the questions below, using some or all of the quotations above.

a. Explain what you think the writer wants the reader to think about this office. Then identify two quotations that you think best inform the reader about the atmosphere of the office.

b. Explain what you think the writer wants the reader to think about the boss. Then identify two quotations that you think convey a strong impression of the boss.

c. Explain what you think the writer wants the reader to think about the relationship between the boss and his secretary. Then identify two contrasting quotations that you think emphasize the difference between the boss and his secretary.

Activity 3

Look back at parts a–c of Activity 2 above.

Select one of them and write a PEE paragraph evaluating how the writer's choice of language has conveyed the setting, character, or contrast effectively.

Use quotations to support your points, and language terminology to explain the writer's choices. You may draw on the quotations from Activity 2 as well as selecting others from the text. Use the sentence starters below to help you:

> The writer has conveyed the office setting at the beginning of this story effectively by showing a place where people work hard...
>
> The writer has conveyed the appearance and character of the boss in this story effectively by suggesting he enjoys power and his role...
>
> The writer shows a strong contrast between the character of the boss and his secretary in the opening of this story...

Tip ✓

When writing about language, try to use relevant grammatical terminology such as 'adjectives', 'adverbs', 'common nouns' and 'abstract nouns' where you can, to help you explain the effects of language.

Writing about structure

The structure of a piece of writing is like a building. The foundations, ground floor, second floor and roof provide a basic structure of a house. In the same way, a writer builds sections of a short story: a section that offers the opening narrative, one that introduces a layer of conflict or a problem, one that develops this, and finally one that provides a resolution.

Once you have established the sections of a text, you can then identify the changes and relationships between these sections and the effect of these in relation to the writer's intention.

Key term 🔑

chronologically: organized in time order. A text can be structured chronologically in the time sequence that events happened

Activity ④

Before you read the rest of the story, look back at Extract A adapted from 'Business and Ethics' on page 51. Find the opening section that introduces the setting. Then think about how the next section introduces characters and a conflict or problem. The structure so far is outlined in the table below. The sequence of the text orders the events **chronologically**.

a. With a partner, consider whether you can see a key line, shift or a turning point in Extract A. Discuss this and identify the sentence in the story where you think the shift happens. It may be when tension is introduced or a change occurs.

b. Copy out the table below and add your chosen quotation. Explain how this presents a shift in the structure of the story.

c. Read Extract B on page 55. Complete the table to identify the focus and events of the third and fourth sections.

Section	The writer's focus	What is happening	Quotations
'Business and Ethics': Extract A			
First section (lines 1–5)	Introduction of setting	The office is described	
Second section (lines 6–15)	Introduction of character and conflict	The secretary and boss have a conversation in the private office	
Shift or turning point			
'Business and Ethics': Extract B			
Third section			
Fourth section			

Exam tip ✔

When analysing structure it can be useful to see if there is a shift or turning point in a story. Sometimes there might be more than one. This can help identify the writer's focus.

Now read the second half of the story. Here we learn more about the private secretary and see a shift in power in the relationship between Mr. Brown and Sloane.

Extract B adapted from 'Business and Ethics' by Redfield Ingalls

Knowing something of his employer's business methods, Sloane could have amplified[1]. What he said was: 'Thanks to your royal purple, Mr. Brown. You've about cornered the trade.'

'They can't touch it none of 'em, that purple; positively,' agreed the dyer, with much satisfaction. 'But' — and he became confidential — 'between me and you strictly, Domestic Dye Works, they got

5   a mauve[2] what gives me pain.'

He hitched his chair closer and laid a pudgy hand on Sloane's knee. 'I'm going to fire you,' he repeated, with a wink. 'I want you to go by Domestic Dye Works and get a job. Find out about the formula for their mauve — you understand me — and come back with it, and you will get back your job and a hundred and seventy-five dollars.'

10   Sloane started. For a moment he stared at his employer, his face going red and pale again; then he rose to his feet.

'Sorry, Mr. Brown, but I can't consider it,' he said.

'Oh, come now, Mr. Sloane!' protested the dyer, with a laugh, leaning back in his chair. He produced a thick cigar and bit off the end. 'These scruples[3] give you credit, Mr. Sloane, but business is business;

15   and, take it from me, Mr. Sloane, you can't mix business up with ethics. Them things is all right, but you gotta skin the other guy before he skins you first, right?'

'That may be —' began the secretary, as he moved toward the door.

'May be? Ain't I just told you it is?' Brown paused in the act of striking a match to glare. 'You needn't be scared they'll find out where you come from and fire you, Mr. Sloane,' he added, more quietly and

20   with a cunning expression. 'I got brains, I have.'

Sloane paused with his hand on the doorknob. 'Mr. Brown —' he began again.

'Of course,' continued his employer, 'I could make it — well, a hundred and fifty, Mr. Sloane. But, believe me, not a cent more.'

The secretary shook his head decidedly.

25   'What?' roared Brown. 'Y'mean to tell me you ain't going to do it? All right; you're fired anyhow, you understand me.' Then with an evil glitter in his eyes, 'And if you don't bring me that formula, you'll get fired from Domestic Dye Works; and won't get no job nowhere else, too! Now, you take your choice.' This time the match lighted successfully.

Sloane smiled. 'Quite impossible,' he said. 'I was going to resign in a day or two, anyway.'

30   'Eh?' exclaimed the head of the firm, his jaw dropping and his florid[4] face paling a little. In the face of a number of possibilities he forgot the match in his fingers.

'Yes. You see — you'll know it sooner or later — the Domestic Dye Works sent me here to learn the formula for your royal purple.'

And the door slammed shut behind A. Brown's private secretary.

[1]amplified – given more information, expanded on

[2]mauve – a light purple colour

[3]scruples – reluctance to do something wrong

[4]florid – reddish, rosy

Activity 5

a. Now compare your answers to part c of Activity 4 with a partner or the rest of the class.

Notice how the writer uses a twist in the tale to engage the reader and link back to the theme of power introduced earlier in the story.

b. Consider how dialogue is used to emphasize the contrast between the boss and his secretary in the second half of the story.

- Which speaker has the most to say? What does this suggest about him?
- Which speaker has the least to say? What does this suggest about him?

c. Write a paragraph explaining how the second half of the story is structured using dialogue to help the reader understand more about the boss and his secretary.

Use quotations to support your answer, and the introduction below to help you.

> The writer uses the balance of dialogue between the boss and his secretary to help the reader learn more about their relationship and the theme of power in this story. He structures the dialogue by alternating longer sections and short sections...

Evaluating a text

Evaluating a text requires you to make an informed judgement about a text and how it is written. You must understand:

- *what* is happening in the text in relation to the question you have been asked
- *how* the writer is doing it.

You then need to make a *judgement* about the writer's success, with *evidence* to support your view.

Activity 6

Now look at how a student has evaluated the story in answer to the following question:

> A student said, 'This second half of the story shows that even though he thinks he is powerful, the boss is much less powerful than he thinks.' To what extent do you agree?

In your response, you could:

- consider your impression of the boss – WHAT
- evaluate how the writer shows the boss is weaker than he thinks – HOW
- support your views with reference to the text – evaluate the EVIDENCE.

a. With a partner, read the first two paragraphs of a student response below. In each paragraph, the student should:

- Make a point identifying what the writer is suggesting about the boss and power – WHAT
- Use quotations to support this point – EVIDENCE
- Identify the methods used by the writer – HOW
- Make judgements about how effective these methods are in influencing the reader – EVALUATE

I agree that in this second half the boss is portrayed as someone who thinks he has power. At the very beginning of this extract he is praised for the skill of his company producing the purple dye and the writer shows the boss is very proud of himself through his comments about it. 'They can't none of 'em touch it, that purple. But at the same time the writer hints that the secretary could criticize his business and his methods and chooses not to. This is suggested when he says 'could have' but he chooses not to do it.

The boss is a man who seems to be powerful and he talks a lot in this section. The writer structures this section using speech and gives much more of it to the boss than his secretary. This suggests he is powerful. However, his speech is full of words that are not grammatically correct and by choosing this style of speech the writer suggests the man might have some power at work but perhaps he is not very clever. This is good because it makes the reader doubt that the boss is as powerful as he thinks.

b. Look through each paragraph again. Decide which of the points above have been achieved and which need improvement. Copy out the table below to mark whether Paragraph 2 shows these features.

	1. Make a point (What)	2. Use quotations (Evidence)	3. Writer's methods (How)	4. Make judgement (Evaluate)
Paragraph 1	✓	✓	✓	✗
Paragraph 2				

c. Now complete the final two paragraphs of this student response, using all you have learnt from analysing paragraphs one and two.

Here are sentence starters for paragraphs three and four:

The writer also suggests that the boss knows less than he thinks about his secretary...

However the writer uses the structure of the story to reveal that it is the secretary that really has power when he says...

Exam tip ✔

Remember to make a judgement followed by an explanation of its effect on the reader. Some useful phrases are:

- effective because...
- works well because...
- well-crafted because...
- powerful because...

3 What could be worse?

Skills and objectives

- To communicate imaginatively, adapting tone and style for a specific form (AO5)

- To use a range of vocabulary for effect and with accuracy (AO6)

What is one person's dream job can be another's nightmare. Some can't bear the sight of blood, yet other people long to work in a hospital. Some hate the idea of standing on a stage, whereas for others this is their dream.

What would be your worst job? Have you ever experienced a terrible job, either in work experience or a part-time job?

Read through what some famous people have said in answer to the question. Then discuss the topic with a partner.

What is the worst job you've done?

I had to collect the trolleys at Brent Cross Tesco. (Alan Carr, comedian)

Selling double glazing. (Craig David, singer)

Selling water filters door to door. (Bear Grylls, TV presenter)

Catering, aged 16. (Susan Boyle, singer)

Being a cleaner in a TB hospital. (Jo Brand, comedian)

You are going to write your own story using the third person 'he/she', as used in the story 'Business and Ethics' on pages 51 and 55. In your story you should:

● create a sense of place through description of a workplace setting

● convey character through description, action and dialogue

● use varied vocabulary and sentence structures for effect.

Activity 1

Look at the picture and story-starter in the exam question below. Choose one as the basis for your story.

Either: Write a story set in a workplace as suggested by the picture.

Or: Write a story about a work experience that goes wrong.

Follow the sequence below and on pages 60–61 to plan, write and proofread your story.

Activity 2

Develop a word bank to help expand your vocabulary, related to setting. Think back to 'Business and Ethics' on pages 51 and 55 and do the following:

• Make a list of proper and common nouns that are relevant to the workplace setting you have chosen; for example, you might make up the name of the company to add a sense of realism to your story.

• Add some specialist terms that link to the particular work and workplace that you are focusing on.

• Consider some emotions that convey what one of the characters feels about this workplace. You might use your own feelings about the workplace as the basis for this.

Activity 3

a. Jot down a five-point plan of the sequence of events that you will use to structure your story. Use the questions below to guide your planning.

Plot/structure:

How will your story begin? What conflict will be encountered and how will it be resolved? Outline each section below.

> 1
>
> 2
>
> 3
>
> 4
>
> **Ending**

b. Now write the first two lines of your story, immediately placing a character in the setting you have chosen.

You could use the opening paragraph of the story you read on page 51 to help you begin, adapting it to the setting you are imagining:

> In the dingy office of A. Brown & Co., manufacturers of dyes, things were humming. Every clerk was bent over his desk, hard and cheerfully at work, and there was a general air of bustle and efficiency.

c. Now, using all your preparation, write your story.

d. When you have finished, share your work with a partner. Invite suggestions for improving your story. Finally, proofread your work, checking your punctuation and spelling.

Activity 4

Swap your final work with a different partner. Then think about the following questions in relation to the story you have been given to evaluate.

How successful is the writer of the story in:

- creating a sense of place through description of a workplace setting
- conveying character through description, action and dialogue
- creating a clear sequence of events using their plan
- using varied vocabulary and sentence structures for effect?

a. Use a table like the one below to structure your evaluation. Remember to make a few points for each section of the first column and support them with quotations from the text.

	What worked well	Areas for development
Creating a sense of place		
Conveying character		
Planning and structuring the story		
Using varied vocabulary and sentence structures		

b. Now feed back to your partner about their writing, pointing out successful elements and discussing possible ways to improve it.

4 Working for others

Skills and objectives

- To select and synthesize evidence from different texts (AO1)
- To analyse how writers use language and structure to achieve effects (AO2)
- To compare writers' perspectives and how these are conveyed (AO3)
- To write in different forms and for different purposes and audiences (AO5)

Florence Nightingale is one of the most famous nurses in British history. Born in 1820 to a wealthy family, she always wanted to be a nurse, despite her parents' discouragement.

This letter was written by Nightingale to a doctor from a London hospital. She took a group of nurses to Turkey during the Crimean War to care for the many injured soldiers there.

> Barrack Hospital Scutari,
> Asiatic Side
> 14 November 1854
>
> Dear Sir
> On Thursday last, we had 1715 sick and wounded in this hospital (among whom 120 cholera patients) and 650 severely wounded in the building called the General Hospital, of which we also have charge, when a message came to me to prepare for 570 wounded on our side of the hospital, who were arriving from the dreadful affair of 5 November at Balaclava, where were 1763 wounded and 442 killed, besides 96 officers wounded and 38 killed. But oh! you gentlemen of England who sit at home in all the well-earned satisfaction of your successful cases can have little idea from reading the newspapers of the horror and misery (in a military hospital) of operating upon these dying and exhausted men—a London hospital is a garden of flowers to it.
> We have had such a sea in the Bosphorus and the Turks, the very men for whom we are fighting, carry our wounded so cruelly that they arrive in a state of agony. The dysentery[1] cases have died at the rate of one in two.
> We have now four miles of beds—and not eighteen inches apart. We have our quarters in one tower of the barrack, and all this fresh influx[2] has been laid down between us and the main guard in two corridors with a line of beds down each side, just room for one man to step between, and four wards.
> As I went my night rounds among the newly wounded that first night there was not one murmur, not one groan—the strictest discipline, the most absolute silence and quiet prevailed—only the step of the sentry and I heard one man say, I was dreaming of my friends at home, and another said, And I was thinking of them.
> These poor fellows bear pain and mutilation with unshrinking heroism, and die or are cut up without a complaint.

In all our corridors I think we have not an average of three limbs per man—and there are two ships more 'loading' at the Crimea with wounded—this is our phraseology. Then come the operations and a melancholy, not an encouraging list is this. They are all performed in the wards—no time to move them.
I hope in a few days we shall establish a little cleanliness—but we have not a basin nor a towel nor a bit of soap nor a broom. I have ordered 300 scrubbing brushes. But one half the barrack[3] is so sadly out of repair that it is impossible to use a drop of water on the stone floors, which are all laid upon rotten wood, and would give our men fever in no time.

[1]dysentery – disease causing severe diarrhoea
[2]influx – entry of a large number of things or people
[3]barrack – soldiers' accommodation

Activity 1

a. Before you work on this text, you must establish its Purpose, Audience and Text type.

- Make sure you have read the introductory section to the text so that you have picked up any extra clues that might help with doing this.

- Then select the most accurate term from the choices below:

Purpose:	to inform	to entertain		to argue	to persuade
Audience:	friend	colleague		the general public	
	old people	soldier's families		the government	
Text type:	article	letter	report	speech	review

b. The majority of this letter explains the difficulties the nurses are facing. Work logically through the passage, paragraph by paragraph, and list four challenges the medical staff face, using your own words. One example is done for you:

> The huge numbers of sick and wounded men that continue to increase.

c. Nightingale uses examples of descriptive and emotive language to emphasize the difficulty of her role. Select three examples of this and explain their effect. One example is done for you – use the same sentence starters in your own answers.

> Nightingale uses adjectives and adverbs to describe the sick men and where they have come from, for example 'severely wounded' and 'dreadful affair'. The adverb 'severely' and the adjective 'dreadful' emphasize how extreme their experiences continue to be.

d. Nightingale also uses specialist language in writing to her colleague, a doctor. List four examples of such language that show she is knowledgeable about her job.

e. Drawing on your notes above, write three points using the PEE (Point, Evidence, Explanation) structure to explain how Nightingale uses language to inform and interest her colleague about her work during the Crimean War.

How writers use structure

In the 21st century, medics and patients are still battling against physical and funding difficulties across the world.

One famous author who has seen this first hand is Neil Gaiman. He works with the United Nations Refugee Agency 'UNHCR' and has made fundraising videos for them. Read the final section of a report he wrote for *The Guardian* newspaper about his trip to a refugee camp.

Neil Gaiman visits a refugee camp in Jordan

I look at Azraq camp, with room for another 126,000 people, all of whom will come, most of whom will risk death to get there, and I know that is another 126,000 nightmares.

5 I realize I have stopped thinking about political divides, about freedom fighters or terrorists, about dictators and armies. I am thinking only of the fragility of civilization. The lives the refugees had were our lives:
10 they owned corner shops and sold cars, they farmed or worked in factories or owned factories or sold insurance. None of them expected to be running for their lives, leaving everything they had because
15 they had nothing to come back to, making smuggled border crossings, walking past the dismembered corpses of other people who had tried to make the crossing but had been caught or been betrayed.

I keep going, talking to the refugees, to the 20 people who run the camps and care for the refugees, and then, after accompanying Ayman, a Syrian volunteer nurse on his rounds, as he changes the dressings on a youth whose foot was blown off by a 25 landmine and an 11-year-old girl who lost half her jaw in a mortar attack that killed her father, I realize I can't think straight. All I want to do is cry. I think it is just me, but Sam, the cameraman, is crying too. 30

I imagine the world dividing into the people who want to feed their children, and the ones shooting at them. It is probably just an artificial divide but UNHCR is on the side of the people who want to feed their children, 35 on the side of human dignity and respect, and it is rare that you know you have picked the right side. You are on the side of people.

Activity 2

a. Read the article above, and identify the:
- **P**urpose
- **A**udience
- **T**ext type

b. Write two sentences to summarize what you think Gaiman's overall viewpoint is about the UNHCR and its purpose.

The extract on page 64 is structured in four main paragraphs. Texts that convey information are often structured in paragraphs. Each one makes a clear point to inform the reader and illustrates the point with further detail within the paragraph.

Activity 3

a. Copy out the table below. Then complete it by:

- matching the main topics in column 1 to the paragraph where they are covered
- adding two short quotations from each paragraph that are used by the writer to illustrate the general topic. Such details are included to inform or engage the readers.

General topic	Which paragraph?	Detailed information
The United Nations Refugee Agency has the right focus		
Gaiman's location – facts about it		
The real-life horrifying experiences of these refugees		
Refugees as normal people like us		

b. Think carefully about the writer's choice of paragraph order. Explain in two sentences how the order of the paragraphs helps Gaiman build up his argument to his concluding viewpoint (that the UNHCR is 'on the right side') in the final paragraph.

Key term

summarize: to give the main points of something briefly

Comparing writers' ideas

When you are comparing writers' ideas and perspectives, you must **summarize** and synthesize the writers' ideas, highlighting their similarities and differences. Start each paragraph with a clear topic that links to the question. For example:

> The writers have different perspectives on their role in these places of suffering. In Text 1...

Look at the outline below of how to structure a paragraph in your own comparison of two texts:

Introduction: summarizing each writer's views and perspectives on the topic

Text 2 – Analysis of methods: how the writer conveys ideas using:
● language
● structure
● tone

Text 1 – Analysis of methods: how the writer conveys ideas using:
● language
● structure
● tone

Conclusion: which writer is the most effective and why

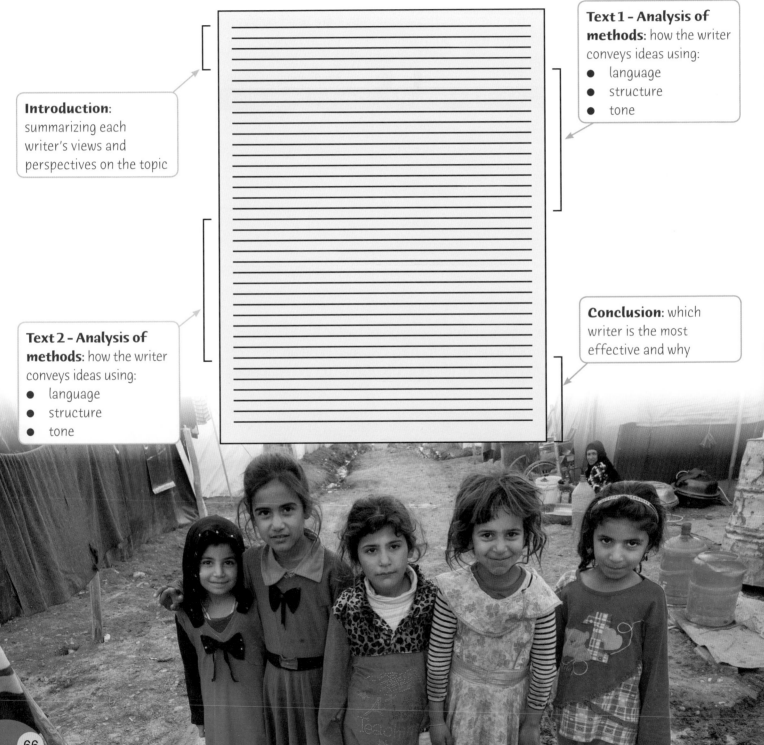

Activity 4

Using all the work you have done so far on these texts, complete the planning for the following task:

> Compare how the writers have conveyed the suffering of others in these two texts.

Look at the features of both texts listed below and identify whether they are demonstrated in just the Nightingale text, just the Gaiman text or both texts. The first one has been done for you.

Feature	Nightingale text	Gaiman text	Both texts
Paragraph structures: moves from general coverage to detailed information			✓
Written in the first person – personal			
Discusses both positive and negative aspects of the work described			
Uses rich, descriptive language including figurative language, e.g. metaphors			
Includes factual information			
Uses second person 'you' to appeal directly to the reader			
Formal tone			
Informal tone			
Emotive language to convey personal viewpoints			
Persuasive language to influence the reader			

Tip ✓

Some connectives for comparison are:

- Similarly...
- Likewise...
- On the other hand...
- In contrast...
- In the same way...
- Unlike Nightingale's text...
- Just like Nightingale's letter...
- Whereas...
- However...

Activity 5

Now look at the openings of two student responses below, in answer to the question:

> Compare how the writers have conveyed the suffering of others in these two texts.
>
> In your answer you should:
>
> - compare the views of the authors
> - compare the methods they use to convey those views and experiences
> - support your ideas with quotations from both texts.

Which do you think is better and why? How far has each student identified:

- the writer's ideas and viewpoint
- relevant quotations
- the writer's methods?

Student responses

Joseph

Text 1 conveys information on the sympathetic views of a nurse during wartime in a number of ways. The writer organizes her information in paragraphs which focus on various different topics. For example, the topic of the first paragraph is the facts and statistics of the work such as '1715 sick' and '650 severely wounded' and the second paragraph focuses on how people back in England are unlikely to understand the difficulties. She shows the horror of the injured men by using lots of descriptive language. For example she describes how awful their experiences are by saying 'severely wounded' and 'dreadful affair' which show that the men have suffered badly.

Tamia

Text 1 is about the difficulties of being a nurse and a soldier during war. The writer says that lots of soldiers are injured. She writes from her own experience so it's easy to believe what she says. But she seems to get very depressed because she says 'wounded' and 'killed' quite a lot in the first paragraph. She describes how the soldiers are suffering in the hospital and beforehand and that the hospital is lacking equipment and cleaning materials so it is not hygienic for the patients. She feels very disturbed by this experience and wants to help the reader understand what it is like. She feels very sorry for the men who have come from the war when she says 'These poor fellows bear pain and mutilation with unshrinking heroism'.

Activity 6

Now imagine you are the writer of the best student response on page 68. Write the second paragraph about the Gaiman text, comparing how the information is conveyed within it. Remember to use connectives for comparison in your answer.

Activity 7

Write a letter to gain financial donations for a charitable cause you feel strongly about. The letter will be sent to parents and students at your school or college.

When you have finished:

- check that you have laid out your letter correctly
- proofread your work
- share your writing with a partner
- discuss any changes you might make to improve your letter.

Progress check

In this chapter you have developed some key skills. Complete the progress check below to see how confident you now feel about applying these skills.

a. Re-read your answer to Activity 7 and check you have satisfied each of the skills below.

Key skills I can:	Confident I can do this.	OK Sometimes I can do this.	Not sure I need to practise this more.
identify and interpret explicit and implicit ideas			
select and synthesize evidence from texts			
analyse how writers use language and structure to create effects			
compare writers' ideas and how they are conveyed across different texts			
evaluate how successful writers have been			
write for different purposes, choosing the right tone and style			
organize my ideas and use structural features to communicate clearly			
use a range of vocabulary accurately for clarity, purpose and effect			

b. If your answer is missing any of these skills, go back and make changes.

Assessment

This section tests all the reading and writing skills that you have learned in this chapter to see if you are able to apply them to different sources.

Read the extract below and complete the activities that follow. From humble beginnings in a council house in Hackney, Lord Alan Sugar made his money by selling car aerials and cigarette lighters and aged 21, launched his own electronics company 'Amstrad'. Later he had his own television business show *The Apprentice*. In 2009, he entered the House of Lords as Lord Sugar of Clapton. The text that follows is Sugar's maiden (first) speech in the House of Lords.

A speech by Lord Sugar from the House of Lords

My Lords, it is a great honour to be speaking here in your Lordships' House for the first time today. I am the new boy on the block; in your Lordships' House, I am certainly the apprentice. I would like first to thank the very hard-working and helpful staff of the House for the assistance

5   that they have given me over the past few months. I take the opportunity of thanking those of your Lordships who have taken the trouble to offer their kind wishes and welcome.

I am, as your Lordships know, Lord Sugar of Clapton. Clapton is in the London Borough of Hackney; Clapton is where I was born, where I was

10   educated and where I started my first business venture. I was born into a low-income working-class family; we lived on a council estate and I was the youngest of four children. In fact, there was a 12-year gap between me and my elder twin brother and sister. I often joked with my mother that perhaps I was a mistake – she preferred to call it a pleasant surprise.

15   Some of your Lordships may not agree.

On the subject of surprise arrivals, I think it fair to say that my appointment earlier this year as the enterprise adviser to the Government, as well as to this House, was not met with a chorus of wild approval. As a realistic person, I fully understand the reaction from certain quarters; it is, after all, human

20   nature for people to form an opinion from what they read in the media or, in my case, what they see on TV. Apart from the wonderful title of 'Lord Sugar of Clapton', I seem to have been awarded another – that of a 'telly Peer'.

With that in mind, those of your Lordships who may have stumbled upon the TV show might recall that, when it started six years ago, I made a

25   statement: 'Never, ever, underestimate me'. As an example, at the age of 16 I failed an aptitude test at the head office of IBM in Wigmore Street, where I had applied to be an apprentice programmer. Twenty or so years later, I signed the licence agreement with IBM, because I had captured from it 30 per cent of the European home computer market. Forgive my little boast,

30   but today I own its European headquarters on the south bank of the river.

My business career started in 1966 at the age of 19, when I withdrew £100 from my Post Office savings account. I bought a second-hand minivan and some stock and by the end of the week I was earning three times more than I would have been, doing the same job for someone

35 else. From that point on, I learnt all aspects of business – bookkeeping, credit control, advertising, hiring staff. I have done my fair share of working on the production line – I have loaded lorries and packed parcels. I did not make my fortune by sitting in front of a screen trading in shares and currencies. The only hedge fund that I ever had was to buy my gardener a

40 new Black & Decker. I made it by fair, honest and simple trading.

This activity will secure your knowledge about how to **identify and interpret information (AO1).**

 Activity 1

a. From the first two paragraphs of text, select four pieces of information about Alan Sugar.

b. What impression does the speaker attempt to give about his character? Use evidence to support your answer.

c. What attitudes to his audience are displayed in this section of his speech? Use evidence to support your answer.

This activity will secure your knowledge about **how writers use language and structure to achieve effects (AO2).**

Activity 2

a. What style of language is the speaker using when he says 'it is a great honour' in line 1 and what is the intended effect?

b. Find two examples where the speaker has used wit or humour and explain the intended effect on the audience.

c. Sugar uses a range of sentence forms. Select two different examples from the text and explain the effect on the audience.

d. Using your answers to the above and any other examples of language that you find effective, answer the following question:

> How does the writer use language to justify his new role in the House of Lords?

Now read the second extract on page 72. It is a speech delivered in 1899 by Theodore Roosevelt, a man who also began life in a humble way. Through hard work and determination he was elected Governor of New York. This is part of the speech he read before that election. He ultimately became the President of the United States of America.

A speech by Theodore Roosevelt

I wish to preach not the doctrine[1] of ignoble[2] ease but the doctrine of the strenuous[3] life; the life of toil and effort; of labour and strife[4]; to preach that highest form of success which comes not to the man who desires mere easy peace but to the man who does not shrink from danger, from
5 hardship, or from bitter toil[5], and who out of these wins the splendid ultimate triumph.

A life of ignoble ease, a life of that peace which springs merely from lack either of desire or of power to strive after great things, is as little worthy of a nation as of an individual [...]

10 We do not admire the man of timid peace. We admire the man who embodies victorious effort; the man who never wrongs his neighbour, who is prompt to help a friend; but who has those virile[6] qualities necessary to win in the stern strife of actual life. It is hard to fail; but it is worse never to have tried to succeed. In this life we get nothing save by effort. [...] A
15 mere life of ease is not in the end a satisfactory life, and above all it is a life which ultimately unfits those who follow it for serious work in the world.

The timid man, the lazy man, the man who distrusts his country, the overcivilized man, who has lost the great fighting, masterful virtues, the ignorant man and the man of dull mind, whose soul is incapable
20 of feeling the mighty lift that thrills 'stern men with empires in their brains' – all these, of course, shrink from seeing the nation undertake its new duties; shrink from seeing us build a navy and army adequate to our needs; shrink from seeing us do our share of the world's work by bringing order out of chaos [...] These are the men who fear the
25 strenuous life, who fear the only national life which is really worth leading.

[1]doctrine – set of beliefs

[2]ignoble – not noble, not possessing excellent characteristics

[3]strenuous – making great effort

[4]strife – conflict or disagreement

[5]toil – hard work

[6]virile – having strength and energy

This activity will secure your knowledge about **how writers/speakers use language (AO2).**

Activity 3

a. Summarize in a sentence, in your own words, what the speaker is recommending as a way of life. Support it with a quotation from the text.

b. Identify two phrases in the first paragraph that reflect contrasting ways of life that the speaker is considering in this speech.

c. In the second paragraph the writer uses occasional shorter simple sentences. Identify one of these and analyse its effect on the listeners.

d. Using your answers to the above and any other examples of language that you find effective, answer the following question:

> How does the speaker use language to try to make his messages powerful to his listeners?

This activity will secure your understanding of how to **summarize evidence from different texts (AO1).**

Activity 4

Using the work you have done so far, answer the following question:

> Write a summary of what Roosevelt and Lord Sugar say in their speeches about how to achieve success.

This activity will secure your understanding of how to **compare writers' ideas and perspectives (AO3).**

Activity 5

Using the work you have done so far, answer the following question:

> Compare how the speakers convey their ideas about work and success to their listeners. Remember to comment on the writers' use of language, structure and tone.

This activity will secure your understanding of how to **apply writing skills (AO5, AO6).**

Activity 6

Using the work you have done so far, answer the following question:

> **Either:** Write a description inspired by the picture below or describe a successful person you admire.

> **Or:** 'In the age of instant celebrity and lottery wins, today's young people no longer see hard work as a way to success.'
>
> Write a persuasive article for a parenting magazine arguing either for or against this statement.

The Paper 1 exam lasts 1 hour 45 minutes and the exam paper is split into two sections: Reading and Writing. It is suggested you divide your time, giving 1 hour to the Reading section and 45 minutes to the Writing section.

Marks:	This section is worth 40 marks, 25% of your English Language GCSE.
Reading source:	One fiction source text from the 20th or 21st century
Questions:	Four questions: you must answer them all.
Timings:	You have 15 minutes to *read and understand* the source text.
	You have 45 minutes to annotate the source and then write and check your answers.
	This allows you 1 minute per mark for each question. For example, you have 8 minutes for an 8 mark question.
What is tested:	Understanding what is stated and suggested by the text
	Examining how the writer uses narrative and descriptive techniques to engage the reader

Exam tip ✔

You must allow enough time to complete both Section A Reading and Section B Writing; they are worth equal marks. *Most* students should start the exam with an hour on the Reading section.

If you have a history of not finishing the Writing question because you spend too much time on the Reading question, you *might* be advised to begin your exam with the Writing answer, allowing 45 minutes for it.

Ask your teacher to guide you on the best method for *you*, based on your previous performance in exam conditions.

Timing is crucial to your success in this paper. You have to read a text in 15 minutes. The exam board provides a booklet of prose fiction passages to use to practise your reading and understanding.

Activity 1

Use passages provided by your teacher from the 'AQA Paper 1 Reading Support booklet'. Practise reading these passages in 15 minutes. Then check if you are able to recount the story and the meaning of what you have read to a partner.

Understanding how your answers are marked

Here are the Assessment Objectives (AOs) that are explored in the Reading section of Paper 1.

Assessment Objective	The reading skills that you need to demonstrate
AO1	Identify and *interpret explicit* and *implicit* information and ideas
AO2	*Explain, comment on and analyse* how writers use *language* and *structure* to achieve effects and influence readers, using relevant *subject terminology* to support their views
AO4	*Evaluate* texts **critically** and support this with appropriate *textual references*

You must explain what the writer means using your own words.

You must select ideas that are stated obviously and exactly by the words of a text.

You must understand what is suggested by the words a writer uses – 'reading between the lines'.

You must comment on how the writers' words work to affect the reader.

You must comment on features of language (e.g. words and phrases), techniques (e.g. figurative language) and word classes (e.g nouns, verbs, adjectives or sentence forms.)

You must comment on features of structure such as sentence forms and punctuation, use of dialogue, and the sequence of ideas.

You must use subject-specific language e.g. complex sentence, exclamation, and direct speech.

You must make a judgement about the success of a piece of writing (usually positive). You must give reasons for your judgement.

You must use quotations from the text or line references.

Key term

critically: giving evidence-based reasons for your judgements. It does not mean to 'criticize' the writer

In this chapter, you will practise these skills and learn exactly how and where to demonstrate them in the Paper 1 exam.

1 Question 1

Assessment Objective

- Identify and interpret explicit information and ideas (AO1)

Identifying explicit information and ideas

Question 1 is worth 4 marks. It tests your ability to find **explicit** information in a given section of a modern prose fiction text. 'Explicit' means that the information is stated clearly and openly, without any need to interpret by 'reading between the lines'; for example 'the hat was blue'.

Once you have re-read the source text in the exam, you have 4 minutes to annotate it and write out your points. Follow these steps to help you answer the question.

> **Step 1** Underline key terms and focus of the question.

> **Step 2** Identify the section of the source text that you have been asked to select from. Draw a box around it.

> **Step 3** Underline key words or phrases in these lines of the source text that answer the question.

> **Step 4** Write your list in answer to the question.

Exam tip ✔

If you select quotations from *outside* the line numbers given in the question, you will not gain marks.

Key terms ℹ

explicit: clearly stated; you just need to find it

paraphrase: rewrite the meaning using your own words rather than the author's

You can gain marks by either copying out short quotations, or **paraphrasing** what the author has written. This means putting the quotation into your own words.

You should aim to copy out short quotations within your answer where possible, rather than paraphrasing, to avoid changing the original meaning of the text by mistake.

Activity ①

Read the source text opposite together with the example Question 1. Notice how this student has:

- underlined the key words in the question
- boxed the correct source text section
- underlined relevant phrases in the source text
- selected the shortest quotations possible to answer the question.

This extract is taken from the opening of Sarah Perry's novel *The Essex Serpent*. The Essex Serpent is a mythical creature which local people say lives in the Essex marshes and hunts for human victims. The story begins as a man leaves a New Year's Eve party to walk beside a river in those very Essex marshlands.

Extract from *The Essex Serpent* by Sarah Perry

A young man walks down by the banks of the Blackwater under the full cold moon. He's been drinking the old year down to the dregs, until his eyes grew sore and his stomach turned, and he was tired of the bright lights and bustle. 'I'll just go down to the water,' he said, and kissed
5   the nearest cheek: 'I'll be back before the chimes.' Now he looks east to the turning tide, out to the estuary slow and dark, and the white gulls gleaming on the waves.

It's cold, and he ought to feel it, but <u>he's full</u> of beer and <u>he's got on his good thick coat</u>. The collar rasps* at the nape of his
10   neck: <u>he feels fuddled</u> and <u>constricted</u> and <u>his tongue is dry</u>. *I'll go for a dip*, he thinks, *that'll shake me loose;* and coming down from the path stands alone on the shore, where deep in the dark mud all the creeks wait for the tide.

*rasp – to rub harshly or grate

Notice how the student has decided *not* to use this quotation. The quotation may 'suggest' that the man's body is warm, but this is implied rather than explicit information. Question 1 requires explicit information so select what is obvious and clear.

Read again the Source from lines 8 to 13. List **four** things from this part of the text that <u>tell you how the young man is</u> <u>feeling physically</u>.

[**4 marks**]

Read the full-mark sample student answer to the example Question 1 below, noticing the skills that have been annotated.

Read again the Source from lines 8 to 13. List **four** things from this part of the text that tell you how the young man is feeling physically.

[4 marks]

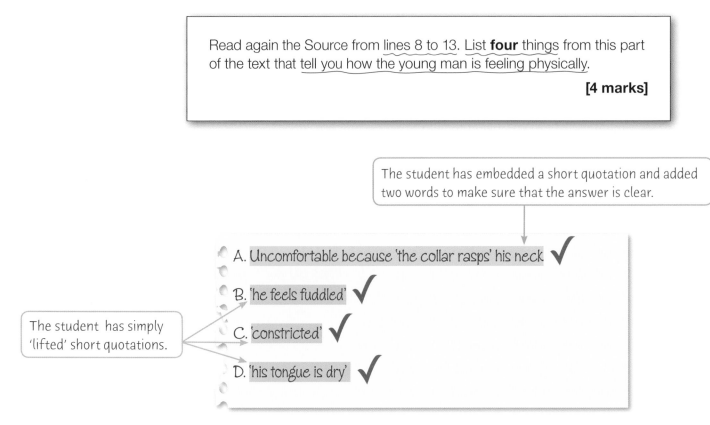

The student has embedded a short quotation and added two words to make sure that the answer is clear.

A. Uncomfortable because 'the collar rasps' his neck ✓

B. 'he feels fuddled' ✓

The student has simply 'lifted' short quotations.

C. 'constricted' ✓

D. 'his tongue is dry' ✓

Try it yourself

Activity 2

a. Before you try out these skills, write down two tips you have learned from looking at this student's full-mark answer. Compare your tips with other students in your group.

b. Now answer the exam-style question below, using what you have learned. It refers to the same source text you just used on page 77.

Read again the first part of the Source from lines 1 to 7.
List four things from this part of the text about the young man.

[4 marks]

A _____

B _____

C _____

D _____

Progress check

a. Now that you have practised the skills needed for Question 1, carry out the progress check below. Consider your answers to Activity 2. Use the following key skills to check each point on your list.

Key Skills I can:	Confident I can do this.	OK Sometimes I can do this.	Not sure I need to practise this more.
identify and interpret explicit information and ideas			
select points that are true and accurate			
select points from the right section of the text			
confirm that the points answer what the question asked			

b. If any of your points do not show these skills, go back to your answer and make changes.

2 Question 2

Assessment Objective

- Explain, comment on and analyse how writers use language to achieve effects and influence readers, using relevant subject terminology to support their views (AO2)

Using language to achieve effects

Question 2 is worth 8 marks in the exam. Question 2 assesses your ability to explain the effects of a writer's choices of language. You must:

- show *clear* understanding when you *explain* the effects of the writer's choices of language

- select and use a *relevant range* of quotations and examples

- use subject terminology *accurately* when writing about language.

The words in italics indicate the skills that distinguish a good response from a weaker answer. You will explore exactly how to demonstrate each of these skills when answering Question 2 as you work through this section.

Activity 1

Look again at the key skills you must show in your response to Question 2. Choose the top five elements from the list below that *must* be included.

- Quotations and examples
- Explanation of the writer's choice of language
- Comments about the audience of the text
- One quotation to support your answer
- Details about the writer's life
- Language terminology, for example, noun, metaphor, short sentences
- Explanation of the effects of the language used
- Comments on the text's structure
- Comments about whether you like or dislike the text

Exam tip ✔

Make sure that any language terminology mentioned is followed by a comment on its effect on the reader. You might use the following sentence frame as a starting point:

Sentence frame: The writer uses [language term], for example [quotation], to create a sense of [reference to the question focus]. This helps the reader...

Example: The writer uses a build-up of adjectives, for example 'eerie, damp and quiet' to create a sense of danger in the house. This descriptive language helps the reader to picture the threatening setting.

Answering the question

Question 2 will present you with a short extract taken from the source text you have read. Look at the following example of Question 2 and the opening of the sinister story 'The Apple Tree' by Daphne du Maurier, published in 1952. A widower begins to feel uncomfortable about one apple tree outside his window, which reminds him of his dead wife Midge.

Look in detail at the Source from **lines 4 to 13.**

How does the writer use language here to describe the apple tree?

You could include the writer's choice of:

- words and phrases
- language features and techniques
- sentence forms.

[8 marks]

Extract from 'The Apple Tree' by Daphne du Maurier

It was a trick of light, perhaps, something to do with the sun coming up over the woods, that happened to catch the tree at this particular moment; but the likeness was unmistakeable.

He put his razor down on the window-ledge and stared. The tree was
5   scraggy and of a depressing thinness, possessing none of the gnarled[1] solidity of its companions. Its few branches, growing high up on the trunk like narrow shoulders on a tall body, spread themselves in a martyred[2] resignation, as though chilled by the fresh morning air. The roll of wire circling the tree, and reaching to about halfway up the trunk
10   from the base, looked like a grey tweed skirt covering lean limbs; while the topmost branch, sticking up into the air above the ones below, yet sagging slightly, could have been a drooping head poked forward in an attitude of weariness.

How often he had seen Midge stand like this, dejected[3].

[1]gnarled – knotted

[2]martyred – showing pretend or exaggerated suffering to gain sympathy

[3]dejected – sad, depressed

In the exam, follow the steps below to help you to answer Question 2.

0 minutes

Step 1 Read the question and identify the key focus the question is asking you to analyse.

Step 2 Now read the extract again and underline three phrases that show any of the following:

- words and phrases chosen for effect
- language features, for example, metaphors, symbols, adjectives
- sentence forms and patterns, for example, complex sentences.

Step 3 Identify any specific terminology you would use to comment on these phrases and pinpoint the effect they have on the reader.

Step 4 Write your answer to the question.

Remember to include the details underlined in the extract.

8 minutes

Step 5 Check your answer.

Establishing clear understanding

Remember, before you can begin to answer Question 2, you need to make sure you understand the question *and* the extract. Don't rush into writing before you are confident you understand both these thing

Activity 2

Work with a partner. Read the extract on page 81 for a second time. One of you should be the 'teller' and the other should be the listener. The teller must:

- explain what is happening in the story
- explain from whose point of view the story is told
- explain the impression gained by the reader of:
  - the apple tree
  - the wife
  - the widower
- give evidence for how these impressions are created.

The listener must check if their partner has understood the ideas in the text and is able to discuss the effect of the language on the reader. Discuss any differences of opinion.

Activity 3

Remind yourself of the example Question 2 on page 81.

a. Copy out the words that tell you the focus of the language you must identify.

b. Below that, write your own definitions for the following words and phrases from the extract. Remember to check the glossary terms to see if any of these words are explained. If not, work out their meaning from the text that surrounds them.

| tweed | resignation | martyred | solidity |

c. Now choose and copy the two words below that you think best describe the overall effect of the writer's description of the tree.

| unsettling | threatening | horrifying | hostile |

| vulnerable | weak |

Explaining the effects of language

To explain the effects of language you must understand:

- what is being described
- the overall effect the writer is trying to convey
- particular choices the writer has made
- why the language used works well to convey the situation, character or setting
- the effect on the reader.

In Activity 3 you identified the overall effect the writer is trying to achieve in her description of the tree. To answer Question 2 effectively you need to link:

- your understanding of the overall effect *with*
- the language features used by the writer to achieve this effect *with*
- an explanation of how these features work.

Exam tip ✔

Remember that you will not be credited for any points you make that refer to text outside the given line references in the question. Only use the section that is specified.

Key term 🔒

sibilance: a literary device where repetition of 's' creates a hissing sound

Now look at the following extract from the end of the short story 'The Apple Tree' by Daphne du Maurier.

The widower has cut down the tree and is pleased to be free of the reminder of his late wife. The story ends with an accident as he walks home alone, tripping over the hidden root of that apple tree.

To answer the example Question 2 below, a student has annotated this extract with some initial notes about the overall effect the writer is trying to convey and the language features used to achieve this.

How does the writer use language to convey the situation of the widower?

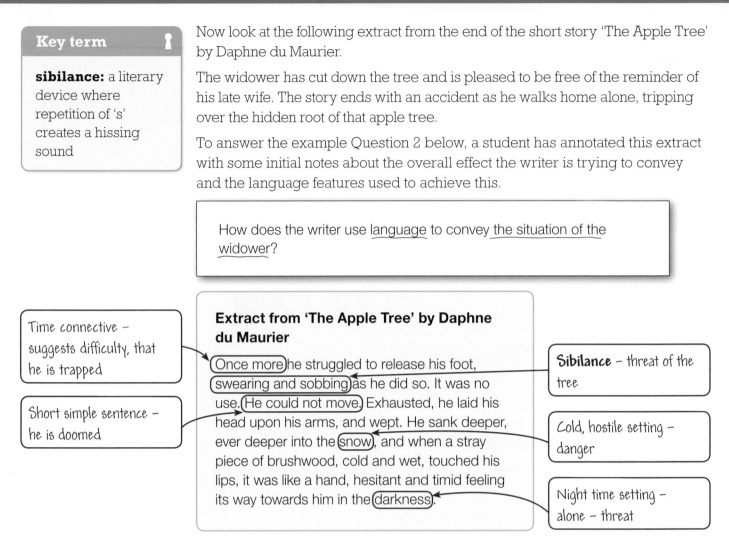

Time connective – suggests difficulty, that he is trapped

Short simple sentence – he is doomed

Extract from 'The Apple Tree' by Daphne du Maurier

Once more he struggled to release his foot, swearing and sobbing as he did so. It was no use. He could not move. Exhausted, he laid his head upon his arms, and wept. He sank deeper, ever deeper into the snow, and when a stray piece of brushwood, cold and wet, touched his lips, it was like a hand, hesitant and timid feeling its way towards him in the darkness.

Sibilance – threat of the tree

Cold, hostile setting – danger

Night time setting – alone – threat

Activity 4

a. Read the two student answers written in response to the example Question 2 above.

Ahmed

The writer shows through her choice of language that the man is in a dangerous situation and he is vulnerable. The writer describes the setting using the words 'snow' and 'darkness' which emphasizes his situation as cold and alone. The simple sentences such as 'It was no use' suggests that he is trapped and he has given up. The time connective 'once more' that begins the extract makes the reader think that he has been trying to get away, but he cannot so he is losing hope. The sibilance in the extract with 'swearing and sobbing' suggests the man feels a sense of threat from this tree, which like his dead wife, wants to hold on to him, perhaps to keep or kill him.

Megan

The writer conveys that the widower is in a bad situation. His actions show he is in a bad situation. For example: 'once more he struggled to release his foot, swearing and sobbing as he did so.' This shows he is trapped. The sentences 'It was no use. He could not move' work well in showing his situation. It emphasizes that he is trapped in a place that threatens his life. It shows that the tree is threatening which is why he starts to cry.

b. Use a table like the one below to assess each student's answer. As you read through each response, place a tick each time you find evidence that shows the student is:

- answering each element of the question asked (writer's language, the man's situation, effect on the reader)

- demonstrating the key skills for an effective Question 2 response (look back at page 80 to remind yourself of these).

	Ahmed	Megan
Uses the phrase 'the reader'		
Uses the phrase 'the writer' or the author's name		
Answers the question by pinpointing 'what' the widower's situation is		
Identifies the overall effect the writer is trying to achieve through language		
Makes a range of relevant points about how the writer uses language		
Uses subject-specific English terminology		
Selects relevant examples (linked to the man's situation) of language from the text		
Clearly explains how the chosen examples achieve the effect on the reader		

c. Do you think Ahmed or Megan presents the best answer? Explain your reasons for this choice.

d. Continue and complete your chosen student answer by clearly explaining the effect of the use of language at the very end of the story.

Selecting and explaining relevant quotations

To achieve your target grade in response to Question 2, you must support your answer with relevant quotations and references to the text. You need to:

- choose the shortest and best quotation that supports your point
- weave short quotations into your own sentences explaining the writer's methods
- pick out particular words to explain in even more detail.

Make sure that the points you make *explain* the effects created by the language choices the writer has made. Avoid making general comments that could apply to any text; focus on linking your explanation to the specific evidence you have chosen.

Below is a good example of how one student, Ruby, has analysed language from the extract on page 84 and used short sharp quotations.

Ruby

> The writer builds up verbs in this extract to show how the man's situation is hopeless, whatever he does to try to escape. For example, 'struggled', 'wept' and 'sank'. The verb 'struggled' emphasizes the physical difficulty of the man and the action 'wept' suggests that the man realizes how desperate his situation is. The verb 'sank' suggests to the reader that he has no control over his body and the landscape and tree are in control.

Point → The writer builds up verbs in this extract to show how the man's situation is hopeless, whatever he does to try to escape.

Evidence → For example, 'struggled', 'wept' and 'sank'.

Explanation → The verb 'struggled' emphasizes the physical difficulty of the man and the action 'wept' suggests that the man realizes how desperate his situation is. The verb 'sank' suggests to the reader that he has no control over his body and the landscape and tree are in control.

Exam tip ✔

Remember that in the exam you will not have time for long, repetitive analysis. Notice how precise this answer is. It has **P**oint, **E**vidence, and **E**xplanation. It pinpoints particularly effective words, then explains their effect and what they suggest about the man's situation.

Activity 5

a. Look back at Megan's answer on page 84.

- Notice the difference between the point in her answer and the detailed point in Ruby's answer above.
- Notice the long quotation Megan uses and contrast with Ruby's quotation of key words, which support the points clearly and accurately.

b. Re-read your answer to Activity 4, part d. Edit it to make sure that you include high quality language analysis in the style of Ruby.

Check that you have:

- used short sharp quotations
- focused in on particular words and phrases
- used subject-specific terminology where possible
- commented on the effect on the reader.

Make any changes necessary to your answer.

Using subject terminology accurately

When you answer Question 2, you must use subject terminology accurately. This means that as well as identifying language features and explaining the effects, you should know the correct subject terminology to name them.

Activity 6

Look at the examples of key terms below and link them to the correct definitions. An example has been done for you. For exam success you must learn these terms and be able to identify them in text extracts.

Terms	Definitions
1. pronoun	**a.** a literary device where strongly stressed consonants create a hissing sound
2. simile	**b.** repetition of initial consonants for a specific effect
3. metaphor	**c.** a word that is used more than once in close proximity by the writer
4. repetition	**d.** where an object is used to represent an abstract idea
5. symbolism	**e.** a word that identifies actions, thoughts, feelings or the state of being
6. imagery	**f.** short words that replace a noun, like 'it', 'she', 'he', 'you', 'we', 'they', 'us', 'them'
7. sibilance	**g.** representing an idea in human form or presenting a thing as having human characteristics
8. alliteration	**h.** a word that is used to modify verbs, adjectives or whole sentences
9. simple sentence	**i.** a sentence which has a main clause (which could stand alone as a simple sentence) and a dependent clause (which could not stand alone as a sentence on its own)
10. complex sentence	**j.** where one thing is compared to another thing, using a connective word such as 'like' or 'as'
11. personification	**k.** a word that describes a noun
12. verb	**l.** a sentence made up of a single clause; it has a subject and one main verb
13. adjective	**m.** a comparison showing the similarity between two quite different things where one is described as the other
14. adverb	**n.** the use of visual descriptions to convey an idea to the reader

(Line drawn linking 7. sibilance to a.)

Exam tip ✔

Remember that any use of literary terminology must be followed by an explanation of the effect of the writer's choice. You will not gain credit for using the terms without explaining how they work.

Try it yourself

Now read an extract from the middle of 'The Apple Tree' in which the widower cuts down the apple tree that reminds him of his wife. His feelings about the tree, and perhaps his wife, are revealed in his actions.

Extract from 'The Apple Tree' by Daphne du Maurier

Up and down went the heavy axe, splitting and tearing at the tree. Off came the peeling bark, the great white strips of underwood, raw and stringy. Hack at it, blast at it, gouge at the tough tissue, throw the axe away, claw at the rubbery flesh with the bare hands. Not far
5 enough yet, go on, go on.

There goes the saw, the wedge, released. Now up with the axe again. Down there, heavy, where the stringy threads cling so steadfast*. Now she's groaning, now she's splitting, now she's rocking and swaying, hanging there upon one bleeding strip. Boot her, then. That's it, kick
10 her, kick her again, one final blow, she's over, she's falling…she's down…damn her, blast her…she's down, splitting the air with sound, and all her branches spread about her on the ground.

*steadfast – firm, unwavering

Exam tip ✔

Using the **P**oint, **E**vidence, **E**xplain model will make sure that you write clear explanations with a range of evidence in the exam.

Activity 7

You are now going to write an answer to the following question:

> How does the writer use language to convey the widower's thoughts and behaviour?
>
> You could include the writer's choice of:
> - words and phrases
> - language features and techniques
> - sentence forms.

Before you start to write, find an example of two language features in this text, using the list of terms on page 87 to help you. Then explain their effect in conveying the widower's thoughts and behaviour. Use short quotations to support your choices.

Point
Evidence
Explain
Point
Evidence
Explain

Du Maurier uses…
For example, …
This conveys the widower's thoughts/behaviour as…
The writer also uses…
For example, …
The effect of this is to…

In the exam you will be given at least a page and a half to write your response. This question requires a longer answer for 8 marks but you don't have to use all the space given; aim for about one side of the answer booklet if you have average-sized writing.

Remember that you must:

- use subject terminology *accurately* when writing about language
- select and use a *relevant range* of quotations and examples
- show *clear* understanding when you *explain* the effects of the writer's choices of language.

Now write your answer to the question given in Activity 7.

Progress check

Now that you have practised the skills needed for Question 2, carry out the progress check below.

a. Look back at your answer in Activity 7. Annotate your answer to pick out the evidence that shows the following key skills:

Key Skills I can:	Confident I can do this.	OK Sometimes I can do this.	Not sure I need to practise this more.
make clear and accurate use of subject terminology when writing about language			
select and use a range of relevant quotations and examples			
explain clearly the effects of the writer's choices of language.			

b. If any of your points do not show these skills, go back to your answer and make changes.

3 Question 3

Assessment Objective

- Explain, comment on and analyse how writers use structure to achieve effects and influence readers, using relevant subject terminology to support their views (AO2)

Using structure to achieve effects and influence readers

Question 3 is worth 8 marks and you will need to think about the whole text. It assesses your ability to analyse the effects of a writer's use of structure. You will need to:

- show *clear* understanding when you *explain* the effects of a writer's choice of structural features
- select and use a *range* of *relevant* quotations and examples
- use subject terminology *accurately* when writing about structure.

Re-read these key skills for Question 3 again. Notice the words in italics which indicate the skills that distinguish a good response from a weaker answer.

You will now explore each of these key skills to help you write the best possible answer to Question 3. These are the same skills you used in response to Question 2, but you are now applying these to the analysis of *structure* rather than language.

What is structure?

You must be clear about what is meant by structure. You should know what to look for and annotate in any unseen extract in the exam. The structure of a text means 'how it has been built'.

With a house this might mean:

What does it look like overall?

- Considering the shape of the whole building.

How is it built? What are its layers?

- Looking more closely to notice the different levels, for example, foundations, floor 1, floor 2, attic, the roof.

What it is made of? How are those components put together?

- Moving closer to look at the bricks and mortar.

With a text this might mean:

What does it look like overall?

- Considering the development and mood of the whole text and its effect on the reader. Notice any change or shift.

How is it built? What are its layers?

- Looking more closely to notice paragraphs, their focus and how they are organized.

What it is made of? What are the 'ingredients'? How are they joined together? Can you see patterns?

- Moving in to look at sentences and their structure.

Establishing clear understanding

Before you explore the structure of a text you must make sure that you understand:

● the events in the whole text – what is it about?

● the words in the text – is there any unfamiliar vocabulary? Is it explained in the glossary?

Then you must annotate the structural features used *across the whole text* in relation to the question asked.

Close reading

In the exam you are asked how the text is structured to interest you as a reader. Here is an example of Question 3, which will be explored in this unit:

> You need to think about the **whole of the Source**. The text is from the middle of the short story. How has the writer structured the text to interest you as a reader?

As you read through the whole text, you should try to identify what the writer is focusing on to engage the reader.

For each aspect in the house diagram below, you must consider:

● why the writer has made these choices

● why and how they interest the reader

● whether there are any shifts or changes as the text progresses from beginning to end.

Viewpoint
Who is telling the story?
Is there any change of viewpoint?

Time
How is it organized? Is the text sequenced by chronological time or are there time shifts backwards or forwards?

Setting
Where does the action or description take place? Are there shifts focusing on one place followed by another, inside to outside, a big picture to a small detail?

Characters
Who is here?
How are they introduced?
Do they link, compare or contrast?

Construction
How are the sentences built? How are the sentences joined together? How are the paragraphs built? Are there links between one paragraph and another? What links the beginning and the end? Is there a turning point?

The overall effect

The following extract is from the short story 'The Basement Room' by Graham Greene. A young boy from a rich family is left at home while his parents go away for some time. He is left in the care of the family butler, Mr Baines, who he adores. He is more wary of Mrs Baines, the housekeeper and the butler's strict wife.

Activity 1

Read the extract below, then summarize the events described in the passage using only two sentences. Compare your summary with a partner. Have you included the key elements of the plot?

Extract A from 'The Basement Room' by Graham Greene

When the front door had shut them out and the butler Baines had turned back into the dark, heavy hall, Philip began to live. He stood in front of the nursery door, listening until he heard the engine of the taxi die out along the street. His parents were gone for a fortnight's holiday; he was 'between
5 nurses,' one dismissed and the other not arrived; he was alone in the great Belgravia house with Baines and Mrs Baines.

He could go anywhere, even through the green baize[1] door to the pantry or down the stairs to the basement living-room. He felt a stranger in his home because he could go into any room and all the rooms were empty.

10 You could only guess who had once occupied them: the rack of pipes in the smoking-room beside the elephant tusks, the carved wood tobacco jar; in the bedroom the pink hangings and pale perfumes and the three-quarter-finished jars of cream which Mrs Baines had not yet cleared away; the high glaze on the never-opened piano in the drawing-room, the china
15 clock, the silly little tables and the silver: but here Mrs Baines was already busy, pulling down the curtains, covering the chairs in dust-sheets.

'Be off out of here, Master Philip,' and she looked at him with her hateful peevish[2] eyes, while she moved round, getting everything in order, meticulous and loveless and doing her duty.

20 Philip Lane went downstairs and pushed at the baize door; he looked into the pantry, but Baines was not there; then he set foot for the first time on the stairs to the basement. Again he had the sense: this is life. All his seven nursery years vibrated with the strange, the new experience. His crowded, busy brain was like a city which feels the earth tremble at a distant
25 earthquake shock. He was apprehensive, but he was happier than he had ever been. Everything was more important than before.

Baines was reading a newspaper in his shirtsleeves. He said, 'Come in, Phil, and make yourself at home. Wait a moment and I'll do the honours,' and going to a white cleaned cupboard he brought out a bottle of ginger-beer
30 and half a Dundee cake. 'Half-past eleven in the morning,' Baines said. 'It's

opening time, my boy,' and he cut the cake and poured out the ginger-beer. He was more genial than Philip had ever known him, more at his ease, a man in his own home.

'Shall I call Mrs Baines?' Philip asked, and he was glad when Baines said no.
35　She was busy. She liked to be busy, so why interfere with her pleasure?

'A spot of drink at half-past eleven,' Baines said, pouring himself out a glass of ginger-beer, 'gives an appetite for chop[3] and does no man any harm.'

[1]baize – coarse thick fabric resembling felt

[2]peevish – bad-tempered

[3]chop – food

Question 3 asks you to think about the whole of the source text.

Activity 2

Re-read Extract A from 'The Basement Room', on pages 92–93, thinking about each paragraph in turn. Make a note of the focus of each paragraph, then choose from the words below to pinpoint what the writer is encouraging the reader to focus on. The first one has been completed for you.

> Paragraph 1: viewpoint – character, the boy
>
>   setting – the house

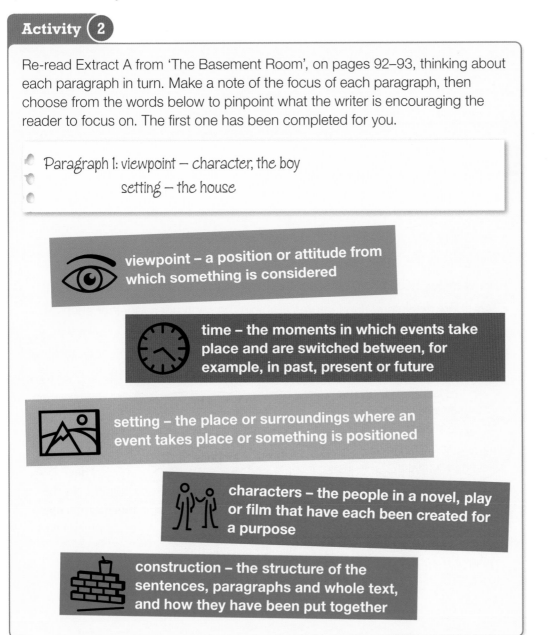

viewpoint – a position or attitude from which something is considered

time – the moments in which events take place and are switched between, for example, in past, present or future

setting – the place or surroundings where an event takes place or something is positioned

characters – the people in a novel, play or film that have each been created for a purpose

construction – the structure of the sentences, paragraphs and whole text, and how they have been put together

Exam tip ✔

Notice and comment on any particularly short or long paragraphs.

- Why has the writer made these choices?

- Does the length of these paragraphs relate to the content? For example, a short, sharp paragraph might emphasize an idea while a long paragraph can be used to develop an idea/dialogue/ relationship/ change.

Construction: How are paragraphs built?

Once you have a clear idea of the focus of each paragraph, you should look carefully at the balance of the text's structure and its shape on the page.

Activity 3

a. Look back at the source text on pages 92–93. Select two paragraphs (excluding paragraph 3) that the author has deliberately presented as short or long. Try to explain the writer's choices and their effect on the reader.

b. Discuss your thinking with a partner or the class. Use the sentence starters below to structure your discussion.

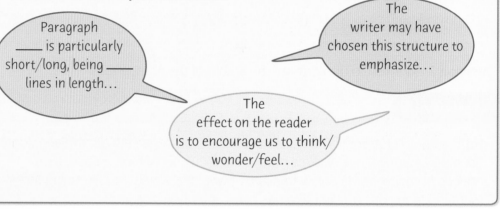

Paragraph ____ is particularly short/long, being ____ lines in length…

The writer may have chosen this structure to emphasize…

The effect on the reader is to encourage us to think/wonder/feel…

Activity 4

Look back at the same two paragraphs you used for Activity 3. Think about how sentences are used.

- Are there any particularly long or short sentences?

- Why might the writer have chosen particular sentence forms?

- How might these choices reflect the meaning in the text?

- Are there any interesting features that join the sentences together such as punctuation or connectives?

a. Discuss your thinking with a partner or the class. Use the sentence starters below to structure your discussion.

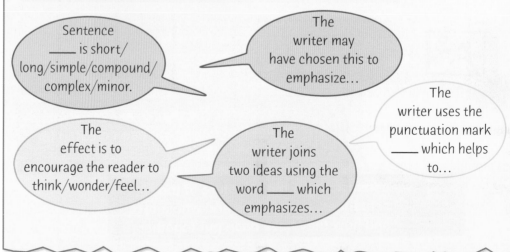

Sentence ____ is short/ long/simple/compound/ complex/minor.

The writer may have chosen this to emphasize…

The writer uses the punctuation mark ____ which helps to…

The effect is to encourage the reader to think/wonder/feel…

The writer joins two ideas using the word ____ which emphasizes…

b. Once you have completed your discussion, select two paragraphs to focus on (excluding paragraph 3). Explain the effect of paragraph length, sentence lengths and punctuation on the reader in your chosen paragraphs.

An example has been done for you, focusing on paragraph 3:

Explanation of effect of the writer's choices

Comment on paragraph length

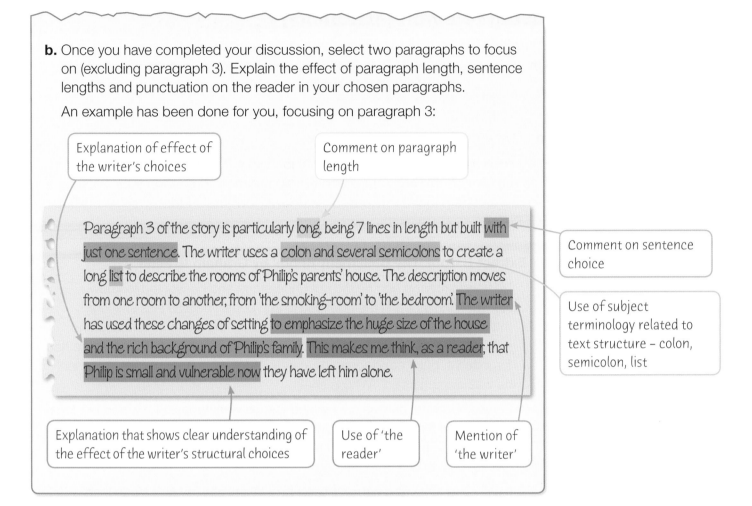

Comment on sentence choice

Use of subject terminology related to text structure – colon, semicolon, list

Paragraph 3 of the story is particularly long, being 7 lines in length but built with just one sentence. The writer uses a colon and several semicolons to create a long list to describe the rooms of Philip's parents' house. The description moves from one room to another, from 'the smoking-room' to 'the bedroom'. The writer has used these changes of setting to emphasize the huge size of the house and the rich background of Philip's family. This makes me think, as a reader, that Philip is small and vulnerable now they have left him alone.

Explanation that shows clear understanding of the effect of the writer's structural choices

Use of 'the reader'

Mention of 'the writer'

Exam tip ✔

Notice in the example above that the student uses the phrase 'This makes me think' to answer the question's focus on the effect on the reader. You can use this personal phrase in your own writing. Alternatively, you could use a more objective phrase such as 'this makes the reader think/feel' or 'this affects the reader by…'.

Using relevant terminology

A writer will use structural features to guide us through the text so when you are writing about them, you need to describe them as actions, for example:

- At this point the focus *shifts*...

  Or

- The writer *contrasts the mood* in order to...

Now read a section from the middle of the story 'The Basement Room'. Philip has run away from Mrs Baines and is walking around London. This section begins as Philip looks in through a café window and suddenly spots Mr Baines out for a romantic tea with a young woman.

Extract B from 'The Basement Room' by Graham Greene

He was inquisitive and he did not understand and he wanted to know. He went and stood in the doorway to see better; he was less sheltered than he had ever been; other people's lives for the first time touched and pressed and moulded. He would never escape that scene. In a week he had

5 forgotten it, but it conditioned his career, the long austerity of his life; when he was dying he said: 'Who is she?'

Baines had won; he was cocky[1] and the girl was happy. She wiped her face, she opened a pot of powder, and their fingers touched across the table. It occurred to Philip that it would be amusing to imitate Mrs Baines's voice and

10 call 'Baines' to him from the door.

It shrivelled them; you couldn't describe it in any other way; it made them smaller, they weren't happy any more and they weren't bold. Baines was the first to recover and trace the voice, but that didn't make things as they were. The sawdust was spilled out of the afternoon; nothing you did could mend

15 it, and Philip was scared. 'I didn't mean . . .' He wanted to say that he loved Baines, that he had only wanted to laugh at Mrs Baines. But he had discovered you couldn't laugh at Mrs Baines. She wasn't Sir Hubert Reed, who used steel nibs and carried a pen-wiper in his pocket; she wasn't Mrs Wince-Dudley; she was darkness when the night-light went out in a draught; she was the frozen

20 blocks of earth he had seen one winter in a graveyard when someone said, 'They need an electric drill'; she was the flowers gone bad and smelling in the little closet room[2] at Penstanley. There was nothing to laugh about. You had to endure her when she was there and forget about her quickly when she was away, suppress the thought of her, ram it down deep.

25 Baines said, 'It's only Phil,' beckoned him in and gave him the pink iced cake the girl hadn't eaten, but the afternoon was broken, the cake was like dry bread in the throat. The girl left them at once; she even forgot to take the powder; like a small blunt icicle in her white mackintosh she stood in the doorway with her back to them, then melted into the afternoon.

30 'Who is she?' Philip asked. 'Is she your niece?'

'Oh, yes,' Baines said, 'that's who she is; she's my niece,' and poured the last drops of water on to the coarse black leaves in the teapot.

[1]cocky – over-confident   [2]closet room – toilet

Activity 5

Re-read Extract B opposite and look at the exam-style Question 3 below which focuses on structural features.

A student has begun to write four points in answer to it. Copy out each of the student's points below. Develop each point into a full paragraph to clearly explain the effect of the structural features on the reader, using quotations or references to the text. Remember to use subject terminology where possible.

You now need to think about the **whole of the Source**.

This text is from the middle of a short story.

How has the writer structured the text to interest you as a reader?

You could write about:

- what the writer focuses your attention on at the beginning
- how and why the writer changes this focus as the Source develops
- any other structural features that interest you.

---

1. Overall the writer shifts the setting as Philip stands outside the window, moves to the doorway and then goes in to the café.
   The effect of this on the reader is to...

2. There is a turning point and a change in mood in the extract at the point where....
   The effect of this on the reader is to...

3. The writer uses an extremely long sentence, building up a list by use of semicolons and repetition in paragraph 3, as he thinks about Mrs Baines...

4. The dialogue in the final paragraph provides a contrast between the child Philip's innocence described the beginning of the extract and the adult Baines at the end. This encourages the reader to think...

Exam tip ✔

The following phrases can be used to comment on structure in the exam. Think about how the verbs shown in italics help you to identify how the writer is guiding the reader through the text.

- The writer *develops/builds*...
- The focus *shifts*...
- The action *moves*...
- The scene *switches*...
- The focus *narrows down*...
- The focus *widens*...
- The writer *returns to*...
- The pace *increases/slows*...
- The writer *contrasts*...

Writing an answer

Now read one student's response to the example Question 3 on page 97.

Jacob

> The writer has structured the beginning of the passage to show that Philip is away from home and is a bit vulnerable in the outside world. For example 'he was less sheltered than he had ever been' which makes the reader think that Philip might be at risk on his own and keen for him to get to a safer place.
>
> The writer structures the whole passage by Philip focusing in closer and closer to Baines, from outside the shop to inside it, and eventually without the girl there so it is just the two of them by line 30. This creates suspense and gradually makes the reader feel that Philip is safer in the shop with an adult from his home.
>
> The dialogue at the end of the passage makes the reader interested in the contrast between Philip and Baines. Philip wants to believe he is still a great person and offers a childish explanation of what he has seen with Baines and the young woman. The writer's ending of this passage with dialogue 'Is she your niece?' shows the difference between the child and the man. Baines is not so innocent but he is happy to agree with the story that Philip offers when he agrees 'she's my niece'. This makes the reader feel sad for Philip and less trustful of Mr Baines.

Activity 6

Complete a table like the one below with examples of where the student has:

- clearly explained how the writer's choice of structural features creates interest for the reader
- selected relevant examples from the text
- used subject terminology related to structure.

Good explanation of how author creates interest through structural features	Relevant quotations chosen	Subject terminology used which relates to structure and atmosphere
'structured the beginning of the passage to show that Philip is away from home and is a bit vulnerable'		

Activity 7

a. Before you complete an example of Question 3 in timed conditions, you should understand the following terms and phrases, and be able to explain how they are used by a writer to affect a reader.

Useful terms and phrases for analysing structure

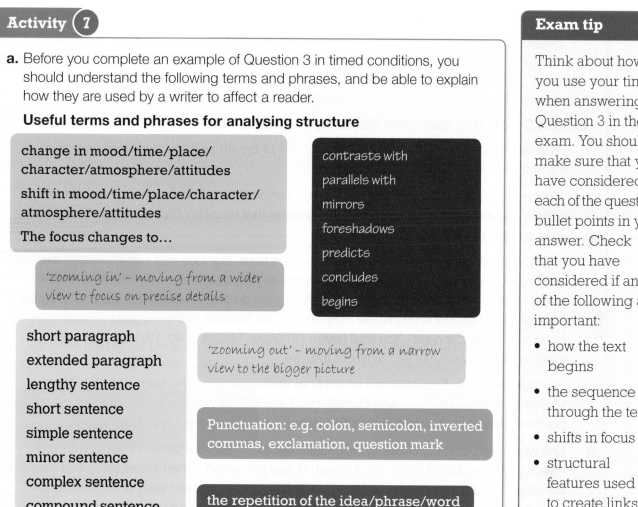

change in mood/time/place/character/atmosphere/attitudes

shift in mood/time/place/character/atmosphere/attitudes

The focus changes to...

'zooming in' – moving from a wider view to focus on precise details

contrasts with
parallels with
mirrors
foreshadows
predicts
concludes
begins

short paragraph
extended paragraph
lengthy sentence
short sentence
simple sentence
minor sentence
complex sentence
compound sentence

'zooming out' – moving from a narrow view to the bigger picture

Punctuation: e.g. colon, semicolon, inverted commas, exclamation, question mark

the repetition of the idea/phrase/word

b. Choose one or two of the terms or phrases and write a sentence of analysis using one of the passages from 'The Basement Room' on pages 92–3 or 96.

c. Learn the terms as part of your independent work towards securing the grade you need in the exam.

Try it yourself

Activity 8

a. Take 5 minutes to read Extract C on pages 100–101. In the exam you must annotate the question and the source text, as shown in Activity 5.

b. Now spend 8 minutes writing your answer to this exam-style question. Remember, in the exam you will be given at least a page and a half to write your response, but you don't have to use all this space.

You now need to think about the **whole of the Source**.

How has the writer structured this section to interest you as a reader?

You could write about:

- what the writer focuses your attention on at the beginning

- how and why the writer changes this focus as the source develops

- any other structural features that interest you.

4 Question 4

- Evaluate texts critically and support this with appropriate textual references (AO4)

Evaluate texts critically

Question 4 is worth 20 marks and assesses your ability to **evaluate** the effectiveness of a text. This means you must come to an informed personal judgement about a text and the choices made by the writer.

To produce a strong response you must **consistently** show that you can:

- *clearly* evaluate the text
- offer examples from the text to explain your views *clearly*
- *clearly* explain the effect of a writer's choices
- select some *relevant* quotations to support views.

Notice the words in italics which indicate the skills that distinguish a good response to Question 4 from a weaker answer.

Evaluate the effect on the reader

To evaluate, you must stand back and look at a text from a distance.

Writers of fiction know the ideas that they want to convey about the characters, setting and situations they create. This is called the writer's intention.

Key terms

evaluate: to assess something and understand its quality

consistently: throughout, constantly

Activity 1

Think about the text as a construction, rather like a building. Look at the constructions below. What kind of impression do you think this famous architect, Zaha Hadid, was trying to give to the viewer in designing these buildings? What was her intention? Discuss your opinions as a class.

In the same way, you need to be able to make overall judgements about your impression of a *source text* and the writer's intention. For example, the writer may be highlighting an important social concern such as poverty, encouraging the reader to consider a theme such as childhood, or may be trying to create a strong mood such as horror or suspense.

Breaking down the question

Look at the following example Question 4. It has been annotated to help you understand what is required in an answer.

> Focus this part of your answer on **lines 1 to 20** of the Source.
>
> A student, having read this section of the text, said: 'This section of the story makes it clear how hard Martha works. I feel really sorry for her.'
>
> To what extent do you agree?
>
> In your response, you could:
>
> - write about your own impressions of Martha
> - evaluate how the woman's thoughts and feelings are conveyed by the writer
> - evaluate how the writer has conveyed her personal viewpoint about the woman's life.

You will be given someone else's opinion. Use this statement to help you build your own evaluation.

You should consider how far you agree. You must have evidence to support your views. You might generally agree but refine one or two areas of the statement with evidence to support your argument.

Understanding the writer's intention

In your answer to this question, you must show that you:

- understand *what* the writer aims to achieve in the passage – the writer's intention
- can identify and explain *how* this is done – the writer's methods
- can select relevant quotations and textual references to support your views – textual evidence.

You should break down each part of the statement and consider how far you agree with it. For example, you could use a table like this:

Student statement	How far do I agree?		
	Agree	Partially agree	Disagree
Idea 1: Martha works hard			
Idea 2: Feel really sorry for her			

Once you have completed a breakdown of the question in the exam, you can go on to consider *what* is being conveyed and assess *how* that is achieved by the writer.

Activity 2

a. Read the extract below and remind yourself of this example Question 4. Consider how far you agree with the ideas in the question.

> Focus this part of your answer on **lines 1 to 20** of the Source.
>
> A student, having read this section of the text, said: 'This section of the story makes it clear how hard Martha works. I feel really sorry for her.'
>
> To what extent do you agree?
>
> In your response, you could:
> * write about your own impressions of Martha
> * evaluate how the woman's thoughts and feelings are conveyed by the writer
> * evaluate how the writer has conveyed her personal viewpoint about the woman's life.

b. Copy and complete a table like the one on page 103 to explore your views. Discuss your answers with a partner.

This extract is taken from the opening of the story 'Weekend' by Fay Weldon, written in 1981. It describes the family life of a couple and their two children as they finish their working week and go away for the weekend.

Extract from 'Weekend' by Fay Weldon

By seven-thirty they were ready to go. Martha had everything packed into the car and the three children appropriately dressed and in the back seat, complete with educational games and wholewheat biscuits. When everything was ready in the car Martin would switch off the television, come downstairs, lock up the house, front and back, and take the wheel.

5 Weekend! Only two hours' drive down to the cottage on Friday evenings: three hours' drive back on Sunday nights. The pleasures of greenery and guests in between. They reckoned themselves fortunate, how fortunate!

On Fridays Martha would get home on the bus at six-twelve and prepare tea and sandwiches for the family: then she would strip four beds and put the sheets and quilt covers in the washing machine for
10 Monday: take the country bedding from the airing basket, plus the books and the games, plus the weekend food – acquired at intervals throughout the week, to lessen the load – plus her own folder of work from the office, plus Martin's drawing materials (she was a market researcher in an advertising agency, he a freelance designer) plus hairbrushes, jeans, spare T-shirts, Jolyon's antibiotics (he suffered from sore throats), Jenny's recorder, Jasper's cassette player and so on – ah, the so on! – and would pack them all,
15 skilfully and quickly, into the boot. Very little could be left in the cottage during the week. ('An open invitation to burglars': Martin.) Then Martha would run round the house tidying and wiping, doing this and that, finding the cat at one neighbour's and delivering it to another, while the others ate their tea; and would usually, proudly, have everything finished by the time they had eaten their fill. Martin would just catch the BBC2 news, while Martha cleared away the tea table, and the children tossed up for the best positions in the car.
20 'Martha,' said Martin, tonight, 'you ought to get Mrs Hodder to do more. She takes advantage of you.'

Identifying and explaining the writer's methods

Look at the annotations that one student has made about his impressions of Martha in paragraph 1 of the source text, below.

Notice how the following has been annotated:

● what is being conveyed about Martha (red text)

● how it is being conveyed (green text).

> She is responsible for everything. The subject of the sentence 'Martha' emphasizes this.

> The family think it is simple. The simple sentence begins the paragraph.

By seven-thirty they were ready to go. Martha had everything packed into the car and the three children appropriately dressed and in the back seat, complete with educational games and wholewheat biscuits. When everything was ready in the car Martin would switch off the television, come downstairs, lock up the house, front and back, and take the wheel.

> Child-rearing is taken very seriously. Adjectives suggest Martha does everything to a high standard.

> Husband-wife jobs are imbalanced and Martha is doing everything. Time connective 'when' contrasts all the activity with Martin watching TV. Sentence 2 contrasts with sentence 3.

> Their roles are traditional. Martin's actions suggest ownership.

> Martha is doing everything for the family as well as a paid job. Opening establishes Martha is over-worked.

In the exam, the student statement presented in Question 4 could focus on different aspects of the source text, for example, the writer's creation of:

Although the question asks you 'to what extent' you agree with the student statement, you can assume that the statement made is a reasonable one that can be supported with evidence from the text. For this reason, interpret the question as an invitation to explain why you agree.

In the example opposite, the focus is on the writer's presentation of Martha's family life. The following features can be used by a writer to convey someone's life:

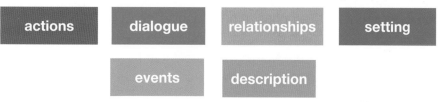

Think about how these features are supported by a range of language and structural features to reveal Martha's thoughts and feelings, her relationships, and lifestyle.

> **Exam tip** ✔
>
> When answering Question 4 in the exam, look for examples of these different techniques. You may not find every technique in the specified section of the source text you have been given, but this can help you to focus on relevant examples which will help you to answer the question.

105

Activity 3

a. Now look back at the full extract on page 104. Identify quotations that you feel convey something about Martha's life. Copy and complete the table below to identify what is being conveyed and the effect on the reader.

Line number	What is being conveyed about how hard Martha works?	How is it being conveyed?
5-6	1 She is responsible for 'pleasure' of others.	Exclamation 'Weekend!'
	2	
	3	
	4	

Line number	Why might a reader feel sorry for her?	How is it being conveyed?
	1 She does what her husband wants.	
	2	
	3	
	4	

Once this has been completed, you should have considered the student's statement from Activity 2, and your own reading of the text.

b. Look at the suggestions below related to the writer's choices and viewpoint. With a partner, decide whether they are true or false. Discuss your decisions, using evidence, with the class.

The writer's choices and influence on the reader	True	False
Weldon shows her negative views about Martha's life by suggesting her life is too busy.		
Weldon implies that the children are lazy.		
Weldon deliberately mentions that Martha also has paid employment, to emphasize the unfair division of work at home.		
Weldon conveys a negative perspective on Martha's life by listing the jobs that she completed alone.		
Weldon emphasizes the imbalance in Martha and Martin's relationship by contrasting his TV watching with her list of tasks.		
Weldon uses Mrs Hodder to show that Martha is looked after well by her husband.		
Weldon uses structure to emphasize how tiring Martha's life is by the length of paragraph 3.		
Weldon uses the quotes from Martin to suggest that his words are obeyed. His advice and opinions, using brackets, suggests he is interfering.		
Weldon uses **irony** to suggest that this is far from an ideal life, even though Martha's viewpoint uses words to describe it as ideal.		

Key term

irony: the technique of using words to convey a meaning that is the opposite of their literal meaning

Exam tip ✔

Do not comment on what is *not* in the text. You are analysing the tools used by the writer, rather than commenting on what is not there. If a device is not used, you do not usually need to mention it.

Writing your answer

In the exam you could be given up to three and a half pages to write your response to Question 4, but you do not have to use all this space. If you stick to the suggested timings, you will have 20 minutes to write your answer. This will give you enough time to do the following:

Introduction	Write a one-sentence introduction – make an overall general statement linked to the question focus.
	State your personal judgement about how far you agree with the student's statement.
	Explain your response to the text in relation to any key words in the question, e.g. if you need to explain the particular mood that is established, or describe what exactly is shocking.

Four points	Write your four points. Each point should:
	• link to the reader's statement and the writer's technique **(P)**
	• link each to clear evidence from the text **(E)**
	• explain why the evidence is effective **(E)**.

Conclusion	Write a brief conclusion – summarize your overall evaluation of the writer's success in achieving the stated aim.

Exam tip ✔

- Balance your response by commenting on the effectiveness of features of language and structure.
- Aim to write four points in this format. You could try to write two on language and two on structure.

Read 'Dark Christmas' by Jeanette Winterson on pages 108–109 and look at the exam-style Question 4 below.

Focus your answer on **line 5 to the end of the Source**.

A reviewer said: 'The extract gradually takes a darker and more disturbing tone.'

To what extent do you agree?

In your response, you could:

- write about your own impressions of the narrator's situation
- evaluate how the writer develops a disturbing atmosphere
- support your opinions with references to the text.

[20 marks]

This extract is an early section from a supernatural story by Jeanette Winterson. The narrator has gone to a holiday house where her friends are joining her the next day.

Extract from 'Dark Christmas' by Jeanette Winterson

The kitchen was cheerful enough once I had got the fire going and the radio playing while I unpacked our festive supplies. I checked my phone – no signal. Still, I knew the time of the train tomorrow and it was a relief to feel that the world had gone away. I put my food in the oven to heat up, poured a glass of wine and went upstairs to find myself a bedroom.

5   The first landing had three bedrooms leading off it. Each had a moth-eaten rug, a metal bed and a mahogany chest of drawers. At the far end of the landing was a second set of stairs up to the attic floor.

I am not romantic about maids' rooms or nurseries but there was something about that second set of stairs that made me hesitate. The landing was bright in the sudden way of
10   late sun on a winter's afternoon. Yet the light ended abruptly at the foot of the stairs as though it couldn't go any farther. I didn't want to be near that set of stairs, so I chose the room at the front of the house.

As I went back downstairs to bring up my bag, the house bell started to ring, its jerky, metallic hammers sounding somewhere in the guts of the house. I was surprised but
15   not alarmed. I expected the housekeeper. I opened the door. There was no one there. I went down the steps and looked round. I admit I was frightened. The night was clear and soundless. There was no car in the distance. No footsteps walking away. Determined to conquer my fear, I walked up and down outside for a few minutes. Then, turning back to the house, I saw it; the bell wire ran along the side of the house under
20   a sheltering gutter. Perhaps thirty or forty bats were dangling upside down on the vibrating wire. The same number swooped and swerved in a dark mass. Obviously their movement on the wire had set off the bell. I like bats. Clever bats. Good. Now supper.

I ate. I drank. I wondered why love is so hard and life is so short. I went to bed. The room was warmer now and I was ready to sleep. The sound of the sea ebbed[1] into the
25   flow of my dreams.

I woke from a dead sleep in dead darkness to hear... what? What can I hear? It sounded like a ball bearing² or a marble rolling on the bare floor above my head. It rolled hard on hard then hit the wall. Then it rolled again in the other direction. This might not have mattered except that the other direction was uphill. Things can come loose and roll
30 downwards but they cannot come loose and roll up. Unless someone...

That thought was so unwelcome that I dismissed it along with the law of gravity. Whatever was rolling over my head must be a natural dislodging. The house was draughty and unused. The attics were under the eaves where any kind of weather might get in. Weather or an animal. Remember the bats. I pulled the covers up to my eyebrows and pretended not to listen.

35 There it was again: hard on hard on hit on pause on roll.

I waited for sleep, waiting for daylight.

We are lucky, even the worst of us, because daylight comes.

¹ebbed – fell back (often refers to a tide)   ²ball bearing – a small solid metal ball

Activity 4

a. Read one student's response below from an answer to the exam-style question on page 107:

Helen

> By the second paragraph, the writer is spooked out by the house and the rooms up the stairs, 'I didn't want to be near that set of stairs'. The sudden noise of a bell begins a real change in the mood of the writing and the narrator describes that she is surprised: 'Surprised but not alarmed'. This paragraph is longer and the narrator shares her paranoid thoughts. The narrator is just a bit nervous and she realizes she has made a mistake.

Check which of the following has been fully achieved by this student. You might want to create a table like the one below to check each element.

a. Clear points that give the student's personal judgement responding to the reader statement	
b. Clear comment on the writer's use of devices	
c. Use of relevant textual references	
d. Mention of the effect of these on the reader	
e. Use of the key words in the question	
f. Logical working through the passage section by section	

b. Write some clear teacher feedback for this student outlining what he or she has done well and key areas for improvement.

Activity 5

a. Read the source text and identify the quotations that you would choose to agree with the statement that the text 'gradually becomes more disturbing'.

b. Now identify quotations that convey a dark and disturbing tone. Notice if there are more of these at the beginning, middle or end of the extract.

c. Decide to what extent you agree that the writer gradually takes a darker and more disturbing tone. Copy the scale below, mark your personal judgement on it and be able to justify your choices to the class.

Agree a little									Strongly agree
1	2	3	4	5	6	7	8	9	10

d. Note down any devices being used by the writer in your quotations and elsewhere in the source text, and explain how these affect the reader. Use the following prompts to help you:

language features

structural features

narrative perspective

mood and atmosphere

thoughts and feelings

actions

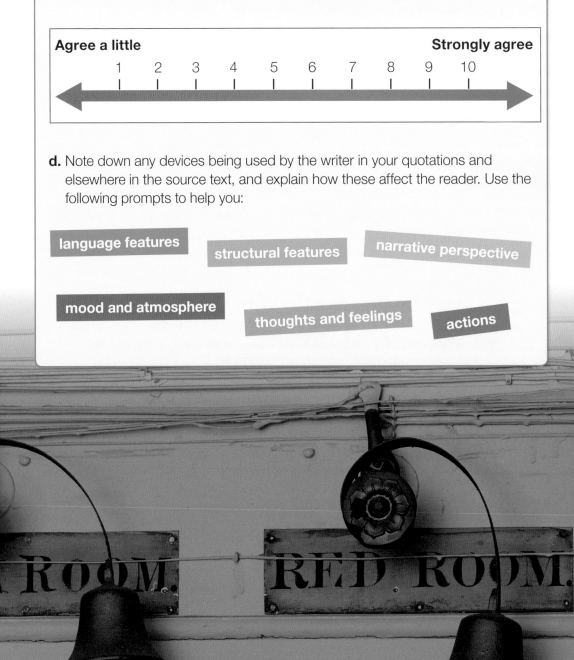

Activity 6

Write your full answer to the example Question 4 below.

A reviewer said: 'The extract gradually takes a darker and more disturbing tone.'

To what extent do you agree?

In your response, you could:

- write about your own impressions of the narrator's situation
- evaluate how the writer develops a disturbing atmosphere
- support your opinions with references to the text.

[20 marks]

Progress check

Now that you have practised the skills needed for Question 4, carry out the progress check below.

a. Use four highlighter pens of different colours to highlight passages of your answer in Activity 6 to show where you have satisfied each of the key skills below.

Key Skills I can:	Confident I can do this.	OK Sometimes I can do this.	Not sure I need to practise this more.
evaluate *clearly* the effects of the text on the reader			
show a *clear* understanding of the writer's methods			
make a *clear* and *relevant* response to the focus of the statement			
select and use a *range* of *relevant* quotations and examples.			

b. If any of your points do not match these skills, go back to your answer and make changes.

Exam tip ✔

Value your own life experiences and use these in your writing. Your reader, the examiner, will have had very different life experiences. For them, a view into the lives and experiences of modern young people can be interesting to read, if you craft it well.

Section B, the Writing section of Paper 1, is worth 40 marks, the same as the Reading section. You should expect to spend about 45 minutes on your writing, splitting this into three stages:

- planning (5–10 minutes)

- writing (30–35 minutes)

- checking, proofreading and making final improvements (5 minutes).

The exam paper will present you with a choice from one of the following combinations:

a narrative task and a descriptive task   two narrative tasks

two descriptive tasks

This means that you must develop your skills in both narrative writing and descriptive writing to be prepared for the examination.

- A narrative task is a story or series of events from your own or a character's experience.

- A descriptive task will require you to describe a person, place or event.

Remember you must complete only *one* of the two choices presented on the exam paper.

Understanding how your answers are marked

Your writing will be marked against two Assessment Objectives (AOs) in the Writing section of Paper 1:

Assessment Objective	The writing skills that you need to demonstrate
AO5 (Content and organization)	Communicate clearly, effectively and imaginatively, selecting and adapting tone, style and register for different forms, purposes and audiences. Organize information and ideas, using structural and grammatical features to support coherence and cohesion of texts.
AO6 (Technical accuracy)	Use a range of vocabulary and sentence structures for clarity, purpose and effect, with accurate spelling and punctuation.

The writing question in Paper 1 is worth a maximum of 40 marks:

- 24 marks are available for *content and organization* (AO5)
- 16 marks are available for *technical accuracy* (AO6).

What is content and organization?

To gain good marks for content and organization you need to:

- get your ideas across to the reader clearly
- match your writing to the purpose, audience and text type that you have been given.

You will need to make deliberate choices of language and textual features, so that your writing has the intended impact on readers. To assess this, the examiner will look at:

- the way you use individual words and phrases
- the way you sequence, link and present your ideas
- the organization of your whole piece of writing, and the paragraphs and sections within it.

What is technical accuracy?

Technical accuracy is using words, punctuation and grammar correctly. Your written response needs to show that you can:

- use a range of vocabulary
- spell correctly, including more complex and ambitious words
- write in correctly punctuated sentences
- use a variety of sentence forms to achieve specific effects
- write in Standard English.

In this revision section you will focus on some of the common technical mistakes that prevent students gaining their target grade.

To ensure that you gain as many AO6 marks as possible, make sure that you:

- check your writing as you go and leave enough time for a final proofread at the end
- check that you have used a range of punctuation accurately
- use a range of vocabulary, including some sophisticated words
- write in full, accurate sentences
- use a range of sentence forms for effect
- check your spelling.

1   The descriptive task

Assessment Objectives

- Communicate clearly, effectively and imaginatively, selecting and adapting tone, style and register for different forms, purposes and audiences (AO5)

- Organize information and ideas, using structural and grammatical features to support coherence and cohesion of texts (AO5)

- Use a range of vocabulary and sentence structures for clarity, purpose and effect, with accurate spelling and punctuation (AO6)

What is description?

A description is different from a narrative. A narrative presents a changing series of events that form a story. A description aims to paint a picture of a scene, person or experience in the reader's mind. It tends to focus on a moment in time, or a contrast between two points in time.

The descriptive task in Section B will provide a written prompt, scenario or visual image to stimulate your writing about a particular location.

In this section you will focus on the task below. Using a model from a published piece of travel writing, you will practise some of the key skills for writing a descriptive piece. You will use the model text to consider vocabulary, figurative language, viewpoint, tone, planning a description and structuring a piece of writing. You will then apply these skills to writing a full answer to the task below.

Consider the task below:

You have been asked to write an entry for a creative writing competition. Your entry will be judged by a panel of people of your own age.

Write a description suggested by this picture:

Planning your description

Where are you?

When you write a powerful description you must help your reader understand where it is located. What is the place or situation? Remember that your focus is on describing the location rather than telling a story though you might want to imagine people or situations to give your description a context.

You have a choice about *when* you make your location explicit to the reader. If you want to initially puzzle and tempt your reader, don't wait too long; your reader may lose patience and feel like giving up! Help the reader by clearly pinpointing the location by at least the beginning of the second paragraph.

Read Extract A below from the book *Walking the Nile*, which is a piece of travel writing by the former British paratrooper Levison Wood. The River Nile runs for 4000 miles. He is the first man in recorded history to have walked its full course. The passage describes his arrival in South Sudan, a place of violence and political difficulty.

Activity 1

a. Identify the two phrases where the author makes the exact location of his description clear to the reader.

b. Discuss with a partner what engages a reader to want to read on in this short paragraph.

- What interesting descriptive phrases has Levison Wood included?

- Which word in the second sentence suggests that Wood is surprised by what he finds?

Exam tip ✔

The picture given to you is a springboard for your ideas. You do not need to describe each small detail in the picture. You might use the picture as the basis for your description or just use the stimulus words. For example:

Picture = a crashing wave in a storm, plus

Stimulus = Write a description set near water as suggested by a picture of:

- a storm at sea

- canoeing in a rough river

- sailing on a lake.

Extract A from *Walking the Nile* by Levison Wood

The moment we entered the compound, I knew things were bad. The South Sudan Hotel had been opened in the run-up to independence in 2011, promoted widely as a safe place for foreign dignitaries* to stay while visiting Bor, but as we approached I saw the hotel minibus sitting gutted on the edge of the road, riddled with bullet holes.

*dignitaries – important people

Vocabulary choices

When you write a powerful description of a place, you need to help your reader imagine that they are there. Appealing to the reader's five senses is one way to convey the sights, sounds, smells, tastes and sensations of the place you are describing. Choose carefully and do not use the five senses as a formula or checklist. The vocabulary choices you make should help to communicate the atmosphere of the place in a balanced way. They should be varied and interesting.

Look at the following notes this travel writer might have made to help them describe a place destroyed by war.

> *Place: South Sudan*
>
> *Sights: abandoned minibus with bullet holes, trashed desks and furniture, fire-charred walls, doors kicked in, smashed glass, cash machine (an ATM) pulled out of the wall – hanging like an eyeball out of its socket*
>
> *Sounds: eerie silence, crunching dust on the road under tyres, slow turning of the ceiling fan*
>
> *Smells: heat and dust, old rotten food from unemptied bins*
>
> *Tastes: dust in the throat*
>
> *Sensations: prickling sweat on skin, dry mouth*
>
> *Atmosphere: fearful, uncertain, tense*

Read the rest of the opening description by Levison Wood below.

Extract B from *Walking the Nile* by Levison Wood

Through the gates, the scene was no different. The reception hall had been devastated. Fire had charred the walls and the desks had been trashed. We waited in the ravaged compound for some time before the manager appeared from one of the missing doorways and welcomed us.

'What happened here?'

The manager smiled. 'Come,' he said, 'we still have rooms.'

He led us across the hotel forecourt. Along the verandas most of the doors had been kicked in, the rooms torn apart. The floor was dusted with broken glass from the smashed lights overhead. When we finally reached our rooms, the metal door was hanging off its hinges and a footprint lay where the handle used to be. 'Fifty dollars,' the manager began. I looked inside the obliterated room. No water, no electricity, but it was still the best option we had. 'We'll take it,' I said.

Activity 2

In your exam you must be able to use a range of engaging vocabulary.

a. Notice the descriptive phrases used in Extract B on page 116 that convey a powerful sense of place.

b. Copy out the four words or phrases that you think communicate the sight of this African war zone most powerfully.

Activity 3

Now consider the picture from the exam-style question on page 114.

a. Before you begin work, establish what has happened there. Is it a burglary? Is it a teenager's room? Could it be the room of a hoarder? Make notes similar to those made by the travel writer opposite to describe that domestic 'war zone'.

b. It's often said that 'good writers are thieves'. Can you steal any words from the Levison Wood extract opposite and make them relevant to the picture of the room? Use individual words, but not whole phrases.

Using the prompts in the box, make some notes to help you plan your description as suggested by the picture on page 114. Try to choose words to help the reader imagine the place.

> **Exam tip** ✔
>
> You could draw on real-life experience or imagine it, but remember that if you have never done something, or know little about it, you are unlikely to write about it well.

Place	
Sights	
Sounds	
Smells	
Tastes	
Sensations	
Atmosphere	

Key terms

simile: a comparison showing the similarity between two quite different things, stating that one is like the other, for example, 'The bedroom was like a war zone'

metaphor: a comparison showing the similarity between two quite different things, where one is described as the other, for example, 'the wardrobe was an empty cavern', 'coat hangers swung in the empty cavern'

personification: giving human qualities or emotions to something non-human, for example, 'even the sun was reluctant to enter the room'

In the exam you need to demonstrate that your vocabulary is varied and becoming ambitious. You must demonstrate that you can use some interesting words.

Activity 4

a. Look at the paragraph below from a student answer. Notice how vocabulary lacks variety or sophistication. How many alternative words or phrases can you think of to replace the word 'messy' to describe the picture on page 114?

> The room was messy. It had clearly not been tidied for some time.
> The ~~messy~~ room was not one that anyone would be proud of.
> (dilapidated) (filthy)

b. Compare your list with the rest of the class. As a class, discuss any suggestions that you think are not formal enough for an exam context.

Figurative language

Using figurative language such as **similes**, **metaphors** and **personification** can help a reader to imagine what you are describing. Thinking up effective phrases at the planning stage can help you remember these techniques when you write your description.

Look back at the notes about the war zone on page 116. Here the writer has included a simile to help the reader imagine the looting that has gone on in this place:

> *(an ATM) pulled out of the wall – machine hanging like an eyeball out of its socket*

Activity 5

a. Look back at the notes you made to help you plan your description in Activity 3. Did you include any examples of similes, metaphors and personification?

b. Note down some examples of figurative language you could include in your description. Remember, you want to create a sense of the place and atmosphere in the mind of the reader, so think carefully about the imagery you use.

For example, if you chose to describe the wardrobe using the metaphor 'coat hangers swung in the empty cavern', this would begin to suggest a dark and mysterious atmosphere.

A description of the wardrobe as 'resembling a laundry basket; it groaned under the weight of discarded t-shirts' would create a much more homely setting.

Narrative perspective

When you are writing a description, you must decide on the narrative perspective you are adopting.

You could choose to write in the:

- first person – presenting a single viewpoint from the perspective of the person writing the description, using personal pronouns 'I' or 'we'

- second person – presenting a single viewpoint as if from the reader's perspective, using the personal pronoun 'you'

- third person – presenting one or more characters' viewpoints and written from the perspective of a detached narrator, using personal pronouns such as 'he', 'she' or 'they'.

Activity 6

SPAG

Read the following sentence from Extract C of *Walking the Nile.*

> There was no food at the hotel, so after some time we ventured back into the town centre – fully aware of the risk, with some trepidation.

a. Note down whether the piece is written in first, second or third person.

b. Identify the word in the extract that establishes the narrative perspective.

Activity 7

Re-read the exam question on page 114, which asks you to write a description of the picture for a creative writing competition.

a. List the narrative perspectives you could write your description from. For example, you could choose to write in the:

- first person from the perspective of a parent or landlord
- first person from the perspective of a teenager or student
- third person from outside of the scene.

b. Write the first two sentences for each bullet point above. Then decide which one of these works best for you.

Tone and attitude

A writer's attitude towards the person, place or experience they are describing is revealed through *what* they choose to describe and *the words* they choose to describe it. Now read the following extract about Levison Wood's search for food outside the hotel.

Extract C from *Walking the Nile* by Levison Wood

There was no food at the hotel, so after some time we ventured back into the town centre – fully aware of the risk, with some trepidation. Soldiers, policemen, and hundreds of armed civilians still flocked the city's filthy streets. The market place stood empty – burnt to the ground by rebels in January – and all of the banks had been looted. An ATM machine hung like an eyeball out of its socket on an outside wall.

Activity 8

a. Do you think the writer's attitude towards the town centre is mostly positive or negative in Extract C? Consider the attitude that he is conveying and where it would appear on a chart like the one below.

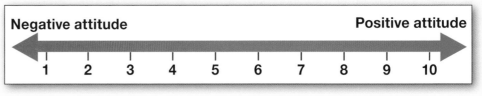

Negative attitude									Positive attitude
1	2	3	4	5	6	7	8	9	10

b. Pick out three examples of words or phrases that establish tone and convey the writer's attitude. Add these to your chart.

c. Continue the following sentence using descriptive language to create a tone of disgust at the sights the writer sees.

> As a battered army truck went by...

Look again at the picture on page 114.

a. What attitude do you want to present towards the place you are describing? Think carefully about the scenario you have imagined as this will influence the mood and attitude of your piece. Write down a word to describe the attitude you are going to convey.

b. Using details from your notes write a short opening paragraph for your description of the place in the picture. Think carefully about the language choices you make to convey your chosen attitude and create an appropriate tone.

Exam tip ✔

Once you have established the main topic and tone of your description, it can be useful to create a quick word bank of varied and interesting vocabulary to support your description. This might include subject specialist words that give specific details about your chosen topic, or **synonyms** for your attitude towards the picture.

Structuring your description

As you plan your description, consider how you can guide your reader through the experience. What do you want to focus their attention on at the beginning of your description? How might this focus change as the description develops? The focus might change when there is:

- **a change of location** (for example, moving closer in to the scene or switching to another area such as from the kitchen to the eating area)

- **introduction of a character or incident** (for example, some brief direct speech, some music, to add details to interest the reader)

- **a shift in time** (for example, moving forward from day to night or from the past to the present)

- **a shift in viewpoint** (for example, cut from one person's perspective to another's).

Re-read the paragraph about the men's arrival at the hotel in Southern Sudan. Notice how the writer guides the reader through the scene, rather like a camera lens that moves across the place, focusing on the outside, the inside and then a particular character.

Extract B from *Walking the Nile* by Levison Wood

Through the gates, the scene was no different. The reception hall had been devastated. Fire had charred the walls and the desks had been trashed. We waited in the ravaged compound for some time before the manager appeared from one of the missing doorways and welcomed us.

'What happened here?'

The manager smiled. 'Come,' he said, 'we still have rooms.'

He led us across the hotel forecourt. Along the verandas most of the doors had been kicked in, the rooms torn apart. The floor was dusted with broken glass from the smashed lights overhead. When we finally reached our rooms, the metal door was hanging off its hinges and a footprint lay where the handle used to be. 'Fifty dollars,' the manager began. I looked inside the obliterated room. No water, no electricity, but it was still the best option we had. 'We'll take it,' I said.

Activity 10

a. Extract B on page 121 contains four points of focus. Each section concentrates on a slightly different aspect to structure the text and interest the reader. What is the final focus?

1. The reception   2. The manager   3. The hotel forecourt   4.

b. Notice how the writer conveys the war-torn area by linking each focus to descriptive details. Copy and complete the table below to identify the writer's techniques to convey South Sudan.

Focus	Descriptive details	What the description implies about the subject
Reception hall	devastated	it is destroyed
Manager	smiled	some inhabitants are resilient and friendly
The forecourt		
Your idea here...		

Writing your response

Now read one student's paragraph in response to Activity 9, written from the viewpoint of a burglary victim.

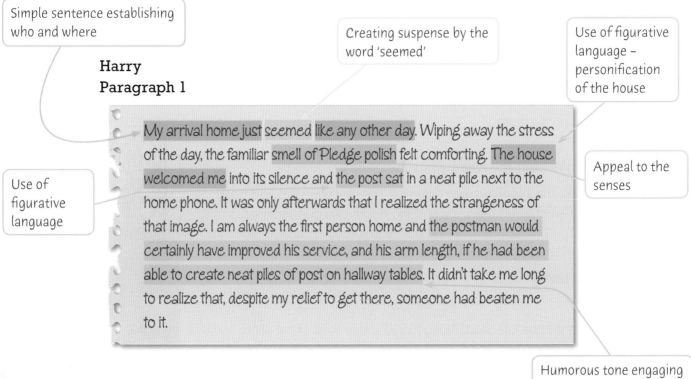

Simple sentence establishing who and where

Creating suspense by the word 'seemed'

Use of figurative language – personification of the house

Harry
Paragraph 1

Use of figurative language

My arrival home just seemed like any other day. Wiping away the stress of the day, the familiar smell of Pledge polish felt comforting. The house welcomed me into its silence and the post sat in a neat pile next to the home phone. It was only afterwards that I realized the strangeness of that image. I am always the first person home and the postman would certainly have improved his service, and his arm length, if he had been able to create neat piles of post on hallway tables. It didn't take me long to realize that, despite my relief to get there, someone had beaten me to it.

Appeal to the senses

Humorous tone engaging the reader

Activity 11

a. Write a contrasting paragraph to follow on from Harry's first paragraph on page 122.

- Change the tone of the writing in the knowledge that there has been a burglary.
- Establish a change in focus in your first sentence by using an appropriate **discourse marker**.
- Describe a disturbing scene as the victim sees his/her bedroom.

b. Check your paragraph. Did you include:

- a change in focus
- figurative language
- vocabulary for effect?

c. Look back at the notes you made in Activity 3 on page 117.

Create a paragraph plan to show how you will structure your response. Each paragraph should represent a shift in place, focus or atmosphere. You could set out your plan like the example below which focuses on a parent arriving home and eventually realizing there has been a burglary.

> Paragraph 1 – Arrival at home. First impression of comfort
>
> Paragraph 2 – Focus on feeling of discomfort moving towards the room
>
> Paragraph 3 – Opening the door – seeing the scene. Focus on smell and atmosphere
>
> Paragraph 4 – Zoom in on particular details – the absence of expensive items. Computer, valuables
>
> Paragraph 5 – Focus on feeling of shock as they back out of the room

Key term

discourse marker: words used to direct a reader through a text. The examples below give examples of discourse markers for contrast, change or time movement:

- whereas
- in contrast
- yet
- on the other hand
- eventually
- finally
- it was not long until
- after a while

Using a variety of sentence forms

You must demonstrate your ability to use a range of different sentence forms to achieve specific effects. For example, you can use short sentences to give emphasis or use longer sentences to extend ideas.

Re-read Harry's first paragraph opposite and consider how *sentence variety* has been used successfully in his answer. Then, turn the page and see how your analysis of sentence variety compares to the annotations at the top of page 124.

Harry
Paragraph 1

> Complex sentence to underline the difference between home and work/school

Simple sentence establishing who and where

Compound sentence to build up details of the home

Complex sentence with a final clause to emphasize threat

My arrival home just seemed like any other day. Wiping away the stress of the day, the familiar smell of Pledge polish felt comforting. The house welcomed me into its silence and the post sat in a neat pile next to the home phone. It was only afterwards that I realized the strangeness of that picture. I am always the first person home and the postman would certainly have improved his service, and his arm length, if he had taken to creating neat piles of post on hallway tables. It didn't take me long to realize that, despite my relief to get here, someone had beaten me to it.

Read through the next paragraph written by the same student below.

Harry
Paragraph 2

It is not long before a sense of unease descends on me and I walk quietly and gently up the stairs. The silence remains. Wondering if someone is here. I have a sense that there is.

Opening the door to my bedroom. Strange that is ajar since I know I closed it when I left the house this morning. As I walk in, the sight in front of me cannot be my bedroom. It is more like a war zone. My scream stuck in my throat as the strong stench of stale tobacco hit my nose. The cupboards had been ravaged and my possessions strewn everywhere.

Activity 12

SPAG

Some mistakes have been made in paragraph 2 of Harry's answer. These are:

1. **Lack of finite verb.** Many students write sentences using the *-ing* form of the verb. This is not enough on its own to secure a grammatically correct sentence in formal writing. A complete sentence requires a finite verb. A finite verb is one that is tightly linked to its subject or noun and may change its form in relation to that subject.

   subject

   finite verb

   Dreary and miserable, the rain running down the windows. ✗

   Dreary and miserable, the rain was running down the windows. ✓

   The day was dreary and miserable, with the rain running down the windows. ✓

2. Change of verb tense. Many students suddenly change tense as they build their writing. For example, they begin in the present tense (I walk, I am walking) and then move to the past tense by mistake (I walked, I was walking, I had walked). You must take care to choose one tense and stick to it throughout your writing. Check on this as you write your answer, as well as when you proofread at the end of the exam.

a. Copy out and correct any instances where verbs need to be corrected.

b. Remember paragraph 2 of Harry's answer has followed on from paragraph 1. What tense is used in paragraph 1? Is the action happening 'now' (present tense) or in the past (past tense)? Is it the same as the tense used in paragraph 2?

c. It is important that the tense established in the first paragraph is continued throughout your answer. Rewrite paragraph 2 of Harry's response to match paragraph 1.

Activity 13

Look back at the exam question on page 114 and the plan you made for it in Activity 11. Now write your own description linked to the image of the room.

Remember to:

- use a variety of sentence forms to control the pace of your description and create deliberate effects
- choose vocabulary and linguistic devices carefully, to establish tone and help the reader imagine the place
- maintain your chosen viewpoint and verb tense.

Exam tip ✔

Remember to refer to your plan as you write your description in the exam. It will help you paragraph your work with one topic per paragraph.

Activity 14

Once you have completed your work, proofread it for errors. Remind yourself of the following key features of good descriptive writing and check you have addressed a range of them.

- A consistent viewpoint ☐
- Vocabulary used for effect and to create a specific tone ☐
- Figurative language used to convey a sense of place and atmosphere ☐
- New paragraphs used to indicate a shift in focus ☐
- Variety of sentence forms used to achieve specific effects. ☐

2 The narrative task

Assessment Objectives

- Communicate clearly, effectively and imaginatively, selecting and adapting tone, style and register for different forms, purposes and audiences (AO5)

- Organize information and ideas, using structural and grammatical features to support coherence and cohesion of texts (AO5)

- Use a range of vocabulary and sentence structures for clarity, purpose and effect, with accurate spelling and punctuation (AO6)

What is narrative?

A narrative, or story, is built from a series of events. It can be real (autobiographical or just based on a true story) or imagined.

In the exam, you could be asked to write a short story, or a section from a longer story, such as an opening or ending. In both cases you can:

- draw completely on your imagination

- use real-life events, characters and settings as the loose basis for an imaginative piece

- relate a real-life story that has happened to you or someone you know.

Whatever your focus, the examiner will look for the following important features in narrative writing:

- a well-described setting

- an engaging series of events which makes the reader want to read on

- believable characters created and conveyed through:
  - physical description
  - thoughts
  - actions
  - speech

- a well-crafted beginning and end.

Look at the following examples of writing tasks that could be given to you in an exam.

Exam-style question A

Write a short story that begins with the sentence 'I love to travel but hate to arrive.'

Exam-style question B

Write the opening part of a story suggested by this picture.

Exam-style question C

Write about a time when a journey began with excitement but ended in disappointment. Focus on the thoughts and feelings you had at that time.

Exam-style question D

You have been invited to produce a piece of creative writing about an aspect of growing up.

Write about a time when hope was quickly followed by disappointment.

Exam tip ✔

Notice that Exam-style question D has a general introductory sentence as well as a specific question. The general statement is wide in its scope; you can make many ideas relevant. For example, 'growing up' can mean 'learning something small' about life or more significant events.

Selecting an idea

You must run through the various ideas you have on reading your chosen exam question and select the best one. Remember:

- Will your answer engage your reader?
- Is your choice one that has some potential for originality?
- Will your answer convey a clear sense of setting, character and events?
- Are you able to draw on real-life experiences, life knowledge or your imagination to bring these to life? For example, if you have never gone skiing, would you be able to write about that experience convincingly?

Exam tip ✔

Some aspects of the narrative task will draw on skills you have already practised in the descriptive writing section (pages 114–125). You are expected to write in Standard English and control the accuracy of your writing.

Activity 1

In the thought bubbles on page 128 are a student's initial ideas for Exam-style question D above. Discuss the suggested titles/ideas with a partner. Using the prompts below, decide which you think they should eliminate from their shortlist. Have reasons for your answers.

- Can you complete the piece in the time available?
- Will a young writer be able to sustain the beginning, middle and end?
- Will it require too much explanation and lots of events at the price of setting, description, character?
- Will it become too silly, inappropriate or too informal for an exam?
- Might it interest the reader through detail, personal experience, emotion or plot?
- Does it draw effectively on the writer's own life experiences, knowledge or interests?
- Does it fit what the question asks?

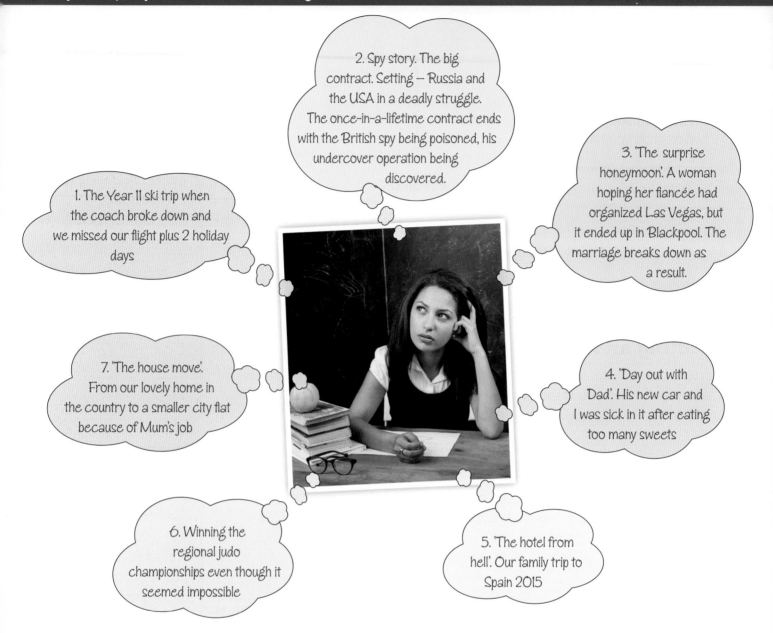

2. Spy story. The big contract. Setting – Russia and the USA in a deadly struggle. The once-in-a-lifetime contract ends with the British spy being poisoned, his undercover operation being discovered.

3. 'The surprise honeymoon'. A woman hoping her fiancée had organized Las Vegas, but it ended up in Blackpool. The marriage breaks down as a result.

1. The Year 11 ski trip when the coach broke down and we missed our flight plus 2 holiday days

7. 'The house move'. From our lovely home in the country to a smaller city flat because of Mum's job

4. 'Day out with Dad'. His new car and I was sick in it after eating too many sweets

6. Winning the regional judo championships even though it seemed impossible

5. 'The hotel from hell'. Our family trip to Spain 2015

Exam tip ✔

Remember, in exam conditions, once you have decided on your story, plan it and stick to it. Working in timed conditions will not allow you to change your mind or divert from your plan.

Exam-style question D

You have been invited to produce a piece of creative writing about an aspect of growing up.

Write about a time when hope was quickly followed by disappointment.

Activity 2

a. Now look again at Exam-style question D. Jot down some possible ideas you could use to complete that writing task.

b. Discuss the possibilities with a partner. Which do you think would work well in exam conditions and why?

Planning your narrative

Remember the narrative task will provide a written prompt, scenario or visual image to act as a stimulus for your writing, so link your planned ideas to this.

Think about the important features of narrative writing: character, setting and events. You want to plan a narrative that introduces and develops these key features.

Exam tip ✔

When you are deciding on the plot for your narrative, remember that the events you include do not have to be anything major. An effective and engaging narrative can be written around the most trivial event. What will help you to reach your target grade is how the characters respond to this event and the way you develop the action to engage the reader.

Activity 3

a. Look at the example plan one student has produced below to help her to write a narrative in response to Exam-style question A:

> Write a story that begins with the sentence 'I love to travel but hate to arrive'.

	Write a story that begins with the sentence 'I love to travel but hate to arrive.'
Character(s)	Two teenagers on their first taste of freedom – first holiday abroad without parents
Setting	Airport Greek hotel + nightclub
Event (problem or challenge)	Hotel so wild – party area – description of music, lights, outfits, etc. – feeling of threat. Surprised to be wishing for quiet
Event (attempt to resolve problem or challenge – might not succeed)	Talk to rep – eventual agreement to move to quieter hotel
Event (climax or conclusion)	Having what you wish for doesn't always live up to expectations

b. Using this approach, plan your ideas for Exam-style question C:

> Write about a time when a journey began with excitement but ended in disappointment. Focus on the thoughts and feelings you had at that time.

In the exam, you could use a spider diagram to plan your ideas for the narrative task. Look at the spider diagram another student has started to help him plan his ideas for Exam-style question C.

Write about a time when a journey began with excitement but ended in disappointment. Focus on the thoughts and feelings you had at that time.

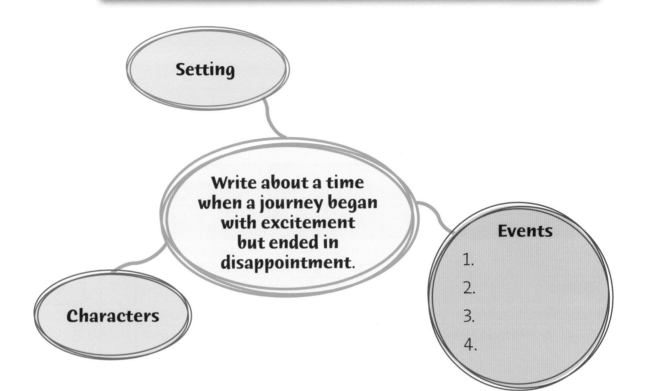

Setting

Write about a time when a journey began with excitement but ended in disappointment.

Events
1.
2.
3.
4.

Characters

Activity 4

Copy and complete the spider diagram above with your own ideas for Exam-style question C.

Write about a time when a journey began with excitement but ended in disappointment.

Remember, you could base your plan on one of the following ideas or use your own:

- a school trip
- a family trip
- a day out with friends
- a day when a major accident happened
- a competition.

Opening your narrative

Whichever narrative task you choose, you need to decide whether you will write this in the first person (using 'I' or 'we') or the third person (using 'he', 'she' or 'they') and whether you are writing in the past or present tense. Once you have made this decision you need to begin your narrative by introducing your characters, setting and an initial event.

There are many different ways of starting a narrative. You could use:

description to introduce characters and the setting:

The hidden meadow felt like the most peaceful place on earth to sixteen-year-old Evie Watson.

action to begin with an exciting event:

The bomb teetered on the end of the wobbling plank... one wrong move and Dexter knew it would wipe the whole street from the face of the earth.

dialogue to let the reader hear the characters' voices:

'Who's my sweet little cherub?' cooed Miss Steggles.

an intriguing or unusual opening line to capture the reader's interest:

Cats don't normally like water, but Prince Samson was a Siamese cat who didn't understand 'normal'.

a short sentence followed by a longer one:

So that was it. Cameron slumped in his seat as he realized he had just seen his last hope of winning disappear in a mere 10.52 seconds.

opening in the middle of the story, mid-action:

George was slammed against the fence: once, twice, yet still he staggered back swinging his fists like a crazy man.

establishing a clear place and point in time at the beginning of the story:

The year was 2016, and on a surprisingly sunny March afternoon, halfway through double Geography my life changed forever.

a line of philosophy or a truism:

'Don't count your chickens before they've hatched,' said Mum.

a question to the reader:

What is the meaning of life? Yes, it's the biggest question there is, but at age seventeen, I think I have the answer.

Read the following openings and then complete Activity 5.

> There's a famous quote I read somewhere. It says we are all given second chances every day of our lives. They are there for the taking; it's just that we don't usually take them.
>
> **James Bowen, *A Street Cat Named Bob***

> Even the dead tell stories.
>
> Sig looked across the cabin to where his father lay, waiting for him to speak, but his father said nothing, because he was dead.
>
> **Marcus Sedgwick, *Revolver***

> The event that changed all of their lives happened on a Saturday afternoon in June, just minutes after Michael Turner – thinking the Nelsons' house was empty – stepped through their back door.
>
> **Owen Sheers, *I Saw a Man***

> Sam is asleep. I could kill him now. His face is turned from me – it wouldn't be hard. Would he stir if I moved? Try and stop me? Or would he just be glad that his nightmare was over?
>
> **M. J. Arlidge, *Eeny Meeny***

Exam tip ✔

It is usually best to write in the past tense. It can be difficult to maintain narration in the present tense.

Activity 5

a. Which of the following techniques has each author used to start their story in the quotations above? Some may use more than one of these elements.

philosophical statement   setting   character

action   dialogue   intrigue

For each quotation establish whether the story has begun with:

third-person narration   first-person narration

For each quotation establish whether the story begins using:

past tense   present tense

b. Pick your favourite opening, the one that makes you to want to read more of the story. Explain the reasons for your choice.

Activity 6

Now look back at your plans for Exam-style question C. Write an opening paragraph that hooks the reader, using one of the techniques opposite.

Exam tip ✔

When writing in the exam, control the number of characters you introduce to keep your narrative clear. Remember you only have 45 minutes to write your response. You might want to restrict yourself to one main character and one or two supporting characters.

Characterization, setting and dialogue

To create a convincing and engaging narrative you need to develop your character or characters, showing rather than telling what you want to reveal to your reader about their personality.

Read the following extract from the artist Grayson Perry's autobiography *Portrait of the Artist as a Young Girl*. Here, he presents his late father and through the setting, direct speech and actions of his father, he shows much about the character of the man and his feelings about him. As you read, think carefully about how he presents his father to reveal character and feelings.

Extract from *Portrait of the Artist as a Young Girl* by Grayson Perry

When my father still lived with us I often used to stand alongside him in the shed. The shed was a square brick extension to the back of the house; it had a window with a bench and drawers in front of it that my father had made. The drawers were painted white, a very thin-looking white, each one having a different knob on it that my father had salvaged from pieces of furniture, to identify its contents. Everything, everything had its place. There were drawers full of brass screws like little maggots, or connector blocks like Lego bricks. My father used to comment, 'The man who invented Lego must have got the idea from electrical connector blocks because they look just like Lego, don't they?' The shed meant my dad and me, just the two of us, together.

To create a convincing and engaging narrative you need to develop your character and the relationships between characters. Perry describes a strong childhood memory of his father.

Activity 7

a. What does the setting chosen by Perry suggest about his father's character?

b. Which words and phrases suggest that the story is a strong childhood memory for Perry? Explain why you have chosen these.

c. Notice the brief sentence of direct speech used in the narrative. What does it suggest about the father and his relationship with his son?

d. Overall what do you think Perry is conveying about his feelings about his father?

Exam tip ✔

Do not write your story entirely in dialogue. Examiners will check that dialogue is set out correctly, but you should also use other techniques in your narrative.

Look again at the sentence of direct speech used in this story. Remind yourself of the rules for setting out dialogue:

● a new line for a new speaker

● punctuation inside the speech marks

● speech marks around the actual words spoken

● use of reporting verbs to show the speaker's tone or actions.

Try it yourself

Activity 8

a. Look back at the opening paragraph you wrote in Activity 6 on page 133. Now write the next section of the narrative in which you develop character and action. Look back at your plan for this task and think about:

• how you can describe the event and show the impact it has

• how you can use dialogue and action to show characters' thoughts and feelings and the way these change.

b. Decide what kind of mood and atmosphere you want to create in your narrative. Think about how your vocabulary choices and the linguistic devices you use can help to create this. Many of the skills you developed in the descriptive writing tasks are relevant here, for example:

• using sensory language or specialist vocabulary

• including a variety of sentence types

• using discourse markers to signpost a change in tone or action

• maintaining a consistent tense.

Structuring your narrative

When developing your narrative, you need to use a variety of structural features effectively in order to gain your target grade.

In the exam, you might use some of the following techniques:

- shifts in time, location or focus (for example, moving closer in to the action)
- varying the narrative pace of the section (how quickly or slowly you take the reader through the action).

Activity 9

Study the picture below and then read the first section of one student's narrative based on this image.

> The first time I approached the cliff edge at Marment Bay things were different. I was a young boy of only six, and my mother gripped my hand in a way that only over-protective adults can. I was fascinated by the sea, and she knew it. She was paranoid about cliffs and edges, and there was no way that I would be allowed any further.
>
> So it was ten years later, with my push bike beside me, that I approached the ragged edge with the faint hope that perhaps, just perhaps, I could creep a little nearer and see if there really were seal cubs nesting underneath.

a. Identify the words in the narrative that show the student has structured the writing using shifts in time.

b. Now write the next two paragraphs of the narrative, using shifts in focus as the narrator moves gradually nearer to the edge. Keep the tension running but avoid getting carried away with any major disaster.

Exam tip ✔

Notice that the focus of the extract by Grayson Perry on page 133 is on a small event that is big in the memory of this narrator. A good narrative piece does not require lots of action and large events. It requires careful structuring and detailed description to show and not tell. It does not have to end in tragedy.

Exam tip ✔

Remember that you need to start a new paragraph for:

- a change in topic
- a change of speaker
- a change of time
- a change of location.

Activity 10

Using what you have learned so far, write the opening three paragraphs of a narrative in response to the following written prompt:

Write a story that begins with the sentence: 'It had been a long wait. But it was definitely worth waiting for.'

(24 marks for content and organization
16 marks for technical accuracy)

[40 marks]

You should use one or more of the structural features identified in the bullet-point list at the top of page 135. You could base your narrative on one of the following suggestions or use your own idea.

- Attending an exciting event
- The giving or receiving of a gift
- Meeting a hero
- A personal achievement
- Visiting a particular place

Activity 11

Look back at your writing for Activity 10. Use the following checklist to check the technical accuracy of your writing and make any necessary improvements.

1. Vocabulary

- Check the vocabulary you have used. ☐
- Underline any words that you consider to be ambitious or interesting. ☐
- Do they help your reader understand your meaning precisely and imagine what you are trying to convey? ☐

2. Sentences

Read through your writing again, focusing on sentence types.

- Do you vary your sentence lengths? ☐
- Do you open your sentences in different ways? ☐

- Does the pace of your writing change? ☐

3. Make any changes that you think would improve the mark this response would receive for AO6. You might:

- change some words to use more precise and sophisticated choices ☐
- replace two medium-length sentences with a short sentence followed by a longer one to create tension or to add detail ☐
- add paragraph breaks to ensure you have one topic per paragraph ☐
- edit some sentences that don't quite make sense. ☐

Progress check

Now that you have practised the skills needed for the Writing task, carry out the progress check below.

a. Re-read your answer to either Activity 13 (page 125) or Activity 10 (page 136) to check that you have satisfied each of the skills below.

Key Skills I can:	Confident I can do this.	OK Sometimes I can do this.	Not sure I need to practise this more.
consistently match the register I use in my writing to the audience I am writing for			
make my writing consistently matched to purpose			
choose vocabulary for effect and use a range of linguistic devices to achieve effects			
make my writing engaging, with a range of connected ideas			
use clear paragraphs and link them using discourse markers			
use a variety of structural features effectively			
write in full and accurate sentences			
use a range of punctuation			
use a variety of sentence forms in my writing to achieve specific effects on the reader			
control my use of Standard English and grammar			
spell correctly, including complex and irregular words			
use a range of vocabulary, including some sophisticated words.			

b. If your answer is missing any of these skills, or you think they could be stronger, go back to your answer and make changes. You could work with a partner to offer each other feedback on your responses.

The Paper 2 exam lasts 1 hour 45 minutes and the exam paper is split into two sections: Reading and Writing. It is suggested you divide your time, giving one hour to the Reading section and 45 minutes to the Writing section.

Section A: Reading

Marks	This section is worth 40 marks, 25% of your English Language GCSE.
Reading	Two non-fiction source texts: • one from the 19th century • one from either the 20th or 21st century
Questions	Four questions: you must answer them all.
Timings	You have 5 minutes to *read and understand* each source text so 10 minutes in total. This leaves you time to re-read when you are writing answers. You have 45 minutes to annotate the source texts, write, and check your answers to all four questions. This allows you 1 minute per mark given in each question, plus checking time. For example, you have 8 minutes for an 8 mark question.
What is tested	Understanding how writers from different time periods and genres present their ideas to influence the reader

Exam tip ✔

You must allow enough time to complete both Section A Reading and Section B Writing; they are worth equal marks. *Most* students should start the exam with an hour on the Reading section.

If you have a history of not finishing the Writing question, because you spend too much time on the Reading question, you *might* be advised to begin your exam with the Writing answer, allowing 45 minutes for it.

Ask your teacher to guide you on the best method for *you*, based on your previous performance in exam conditions.

Understanding how your answers are marked

Here are the Assessment Objectives (AOs) that are explored in the Reading section of Paper 2.

Assessment Objective	The reading skills that you need to demonstrate
AO1	Identify and *interpret* *explicit* and *implicit* information and ideas. Select and *synthesize* evidence from different texts.
AO2	*Explain, comment on and analyse* how writers use *language* and *structure* to achieve effects and influence readers, using relevant *subject terminology* to support their views.
AO3	*Compare* writers' ideas and perspectives, as well as how these are conveyed, across two or more texts.

You must explain what the writer means using your own words.

You must select ideas that are stated obviously and exactly by the words of a text.

You must understand what is suggested by the words a writer uses – 'reading between the lines'.

You must combine and analyse evidence from two texts.

You must comment on how the writers' words work to affect the reader.

You must comment on features of language such as words and phrases, specific techniques such as figurative language and word classes (nouns, verbs, adjectives) and sentence forms.

You must comment on features of structure such as sentence forms and how punctuation affects these, use of dialogue, and the sequence of ideas.

You must use subject-specific language for English, e.g. *complex sentence, exclamation mark,* and *direct speech.*

You must pinpoint similarities and differences in the content and ideas in texts and explain how writers put these across.

In this chapter, you will practise these skills and learn exactly how and where to demonstrate them in the Paper 2 exam in order to achieve your target grade.

1 Question 1

Assessment Objective

- Identify and interpret implicit and explicit information and ideas (AO1)

Identifying explicit and implicit information and ideas

Question 1 is worth 4 marks and focuses on a set section of the source text. It tests your ability to identify:

- information and ideas that are explicit
- information and ideas that are implicit.

Explicit information was tested in Paper 1, Question 1. In Paper 2 you are now *also* being asked to read *beneath* the surface of the text.

Activity 1

Read the title and subtitle of an article about the mountain K2 and its explorers below. Notice the explicit information given about the dangers of K2 annotated.

With a partner, discuss:

a. What is implied about the mountain by the following two phrases?

- 'K2 brings out the best and worst in those who climb it'
- 'Mountaineers risk avalanches, storms, conflicts, and a curse'

b. What do the title and subtitle demonstrate about the difference between explicit and implicit information?

Why K2 Brings Out the Best and Worst in Those Who Climb It

Mountaineers risk avalanches, storms, conflicts, and a curse when they attempt to summit the peak

1. There can be avalanches – explicit detail

2. There can be storms – explicit detail

In the exam, Question 1 will ask you to identify four true statements in a list of eight. Some of these statements are inferred or deduced from the text. You must work out which are true. You will need to read the text carefully and test each statement against what you understand from the set section of the source text.

Here is an example of Question 1, which will be explored in more detail later in this book:

Read the text from **lines 49 to 81.**

Choose four statements below that are true.

Choose a maximum of four statements.

A Houston was an American. ⬭

B Houston eventually succeeded in conquering K2. ⬭

C Charlie Houston attempted K2 twice. ⬭

D Houston forgot to take matches on his first trip up K2. ⬭

E Charlie Houston was a determined man. ⬭

F The author believes Houston was damaged by his
experience of war. ⬭

G The author admires Houston for his values. ⬭

H Houston was an expert in high altitude climbing before he
attempted K2. ⬭

The following steps could help you to answer Question 1:

Step 1 Underline key terms in the question, for example: 'Choose **four** statements', 'Shade the boxes of the ones that you think are true'. This will help you to make sure you answer the question correctly.

↓

Step 2 Identify the section of the text that you have been asked to select from. Draw a box around it.

↓

Step 3 Read each statement in turn and skim through the set section of the source text to identify whether it is true. If you find the evidence to prove the truth of a statement, shade the box on your answer paper.

Now read the opening of a 2015 article from *National Geographic*, a journal for people interested in the world around them. It informs its readers about a book about the explorers of K2 and includes an interview with the author. It emphasizes the savage nature of the mountain and why explorers have found it attractive.

Activity 2

Check on your reading speed and comprehension by reading the article in 5 minutes.

a. Have you fully understood the article on a first read, or do you need to re-read any sections to be clear about its content?

b. Are you clear about the audience and purpose of the article before you begin the questions?

Why K2 Brings Out the Best and Worst in Those Who Climb It

Mountaineers risk avalanches, storms, conflicts, and a curse when they attempt to summit[1] the peak

by Simon Worrall

K2 is 'a savage mountain that tries to kill you…'. Rising steeply above the Karakoram Range along the Pakistan-China border and battered by atrocious weather, this
5 pyramid-shaped mountain has always been the ultimate challenge for the world's best mountaineers—and the graveyard of many of their ambitions. In 2008, in the worst accident in its history, 11 climbers perished trying to
10 climb K2.

[Mick] Conefrey's book, *The Ghosts of K2: The Epic Saga of the First Ascent*, draws on interviews, as well as newly released diaries and letters, to take us inside the obsessions,
15 feuds[2], and acts of heroism that K2 inspires in those who dare to climb it.

Talking from his home in London, Conefrey explains why K2 brings out the best and worst in climbers.

The first attempt on K2 was surely the 20 **most bizarre. Tell us about 666, a.k.a 'The Beast,' Aleister Crowley.**

Aleister Crowley is famous for being an occultist[3]. Some people call him a Satanist[4] but that isn't quite correct. There is no doubt 25 that he was fascinated by the occult and Eastern religion. But although he's most famous for the sex, drugs, and poetry—and for getting his face on to the cover of *Sergeant Pepper's Lonely Hearts Club* 30 *Band*—in his youth he was an ardent mountaineer. The kind of mountaineering he liked was the dangerous kind. He didn't like climbing with guides. He liked climbing by himself or with his partner, Oscar Eckenstein. 35 He wanted extreme experiences where he pushed himself to the limit.

Crowley and Eckenstein made the first attempt on K2 in 1902. In those days, nobody had a clue about what it was going to be like. They thought they would go to the Himalayas and knock off K2 in a couple of days. But as the expedition proceeded, it started falling apart. Eckenstein, the leader, had a bad respiratory infection. Crowley had malaria and spent most of the time in his tent with a high fever. At one point he got so delirious, he started waving his revolver at other members of the team.

American Charlie Houston is a legend in the history of K2 expeditions even though he, too, failed to summit. Why has his expedition retained a singular place in the K2 canon?

Charlie Houston went to K2 twice, first in 1938 to do a reconnaissance of the mountain when he almost succeeded in getting to the summit. But by a bizarre stroke of misfortune, when he reached his last camp, he discovered he didn't have any matches left. That sounds like a trivial thing but if you're at high altitudes and you can't cook for yourself or melt water then life is very dangerous. He rummaged around in his pockets and found a few dog ends of matches. There's this horrific scene where they're striking them and they're dying. He gets to the last one. Is it going to light? Eventually, they got a couple of matches to light but it was not the way to begin the ascent of the world's hardest mountain.

Houston came back in 1953, a very different character, having been through WWII and become an expert on high altitude climbing. The expedition was built around democratic American ideals. He was the team leader but he wanted everybody to have a say. It epitomized the noble ideal of what Houston called 'the Brotherhood of the Rope': the idea that the people you climb with are dependent on you, and you are dependent on them.

[1]summit (verb) – reach the top

[2]feud – long-lasting disagreement

[3]occultist – someone involved in magic or the supernatural

[4]Satanist – worshipper of Satan and the power of evil

[5]canon – a collection of sacred stories accepted as genuine

Identifying implicit statements

An important feature of Question 1 in Paper 2 is that (unlike Question 1 in Paper 1) some answers are likely to contain information that is not stated directly in the text.

Re-read lines 1–10 of the source text on pages 142–3.

Activity 3

Look at the following four *true* statements about this extract.

A People believe the mountain is cruel.

B K2 is situated on the Pakistan-China border.

C The writer believes the mountain has terrible weather.

D K2 is shaped like a pyramid.

a. Identify which answers from A–D are supported by explicit and obvious factual information from the text.

b. Which answers from A–D are supported by implicit information (which means you have to understand what is suggested or hinted)?

Activity 4

Now you can be the examiner. Look back at lines 20–48. Write two true statements about Aleister Crowley using this information. One should be explicit (stated in the text) and one should be implicit. Explain the evidence for your implicit statement.

Activity 5

Now look again at the information on the climber Charlie Houston from lines 49–81 and answer the following exam-style question. Read the text and then time yourself by doing your annotation, answer and check in five minutes.

Read the text from **lines 49 to 81.**

Choose four statements below that are true.

Choose a maximum of four statements.

A Houston was an American. ⭕

B Houston eventually succeeded in conquering K2. ⭕

C Charlie Houston attempted K2 twice. ⭕

D Houston forgot to take matches on his first trip up K2. ⭕

E Charlie Houston was a determined man. ⭕

F The author believes Houston was damaged by his experience of war. ⭕

G The author admires Houston for his values. ⭕

H Houston was an expert in high altitude climbing before he attempted K2. ⭕

Exam tip ✔

When answering Question 1 in the exam, be clear about names and people. Check whether any of the names mentioned in the statements refer to the writer of the text, the main subject of the text or to another person entirely.

Progress check

Now that you have practised the skills needed for Question 1, carry out the progress check below.

a. Re-read your answers to Activity 4. Check each point against the following key skills.

Key Skills I can:	Confident I can do this.	OK Sometimes I can do this.	Not sure I need to practise this more.
read the statements very carefully to make sure that I understand them before choosing			
re-read the text to make sure that I have not misinterpreted it			
work carefully, ruling out incorrect statements one at a time			
check that I have only chosen *four* statements.			

b. If any of your work does not show these skills, try again and improve your answer.

2 Question 2

Assessment Objectives

- Identify and interpret explicit and implicit information and ideas (AO1)
- Select and synthesize evidence from different texts (AO1)

Synthesizing information

Question 2 is worth 8 marks. It assesses your ability to select information and ideas from two texts and synthesize them into a clear answer, identifying differences or similarities between them. One text will be modern and the other will be from the 19th century.

In your response you will need to:

- be clear what the question is asking
- make clear **inferences** from both texts
- select clear references/textual details relevant to the focus of the question
- make statements that show clear differences between texts.

Read Source A below which is a modern text about a young computer hacker who broke the law. Read the text in 5 minutes. Then test your understanding by completing Activity 1 that follows.

Source A

Teenager who hacked governments worldwide is spared jail

A teenage computer hacker who shut down government networks across the world and sent bomb threats to US airlines from his bedroom, has walked free from court.

The 16-year-old from Plympton in Devon began hacking the sites of organizations and governments he disagreed with when he was just 14.

Using a laptop computer in his bedroom, the schoolboy, who cannot be named for legal reasons, caused chaos targeting Iraq's ministry of foreign of affairs, the department of agriculture in Thailand and China's security ministry.

He also crashed computers in the Japanese town of Taiji, where an annual dolphin hunt takes place, and launched a cyber-attack (on) the SeaWorld theme park in Florida almost half a million pounds.

He was eventually arrested after using Twitter to send bomb hoaxes to American Airlines, Delta Airlines and even the White House, telling them: 'There's a nice tick-tick in one of those lovely Boeing planes. Hurry gentlemen, the clock is ticking. High quality.'

After a run-in with a local police officer he launched a cyber-attack on the Devon and Cornwall computer system, causing it to crash for almost an hour.

But when he appeared at Plymouth Youth Court, District Judge Diane Baker said she was sparing him a custodial sentence as it would 'destroy him'.

She told the boy: 'I think you got carried away by the fact you thought you were cool, you thought you were clever.'

'You didn't think of what truly happens in the real world if you do these things. I don't think there would be any positive outcome for you going into a youth detention centre. I think it would destroy you.'

The teenager used Distributed Denial of Service (DDoS) attacks to cripple computer systems by bombarding them with data.

Ben Samples, prosecuting, said the boy was arrested in February last year after the airlines and the FBI deemed the threats as non-credible*.

'Analysis of a laptop found at his address revealed conversations using Skype between him and another user,' Mr Samples said.

'During the conversation on February 14 the boy described hacking as a hobby. He also discussed the possibility of hacking Snapchat and leaking nude images.'

Ken Papenfus, representing the boy, said he had become involved in hacking after meeting people while playing video games online.

He said: 'This was because his friends and his peer group at the time were, as they got older, getting involved in using drugs, using substances, getting into trouble with the police.'

Addressing the court, the teenager, who wearing a white shirt and black trousers, said: 'I just want to say that I am really sorry for everything that I have done. I didn't really know how serious it was. I am sorry to my family.'

The boy was convicted of three offences under Section 3 of the Computer Misuse Act, relating to the DDoS attacks, and two under Section 51 of the Criminal Law Act for the bomb hoaxes.

The judge game him a two-year youth rehabilitation order and a two-year supervision order, and told him to attend 120 hours reparation and two courses.

The boy's mother was told to pay £620 in prosecution costs and the court ordered that his computer be destroyed.

*non-credible – not believable

Activity 1

Summarize the news story using four sentences with accurate punctuation. Use your own words to reflect your understanding of the key events and issues.

147

Now read a court report covering the trial of a child at the Old Bailey, a court that tries criminal cases in London, in the 19th century. The Old Bailey was next to a prison and many people were hanged just outside. The boy's defence was that he didn't commit the crime, but that another boy gave him the stolen goods.

Source B

CHARLES ELLIOTT was indicted[1] for stealing, on the 8th of February, at St. Marylebone, six handkerchiefs, value 1 l., the goods of Martha Blakeman, widow, privately in her shop.

MARTHA BLAKEMAN. I am a widow, and keep a haberdasher's shop[2] in Oxford-street, in the parish of St. Marylebone. On the 8th of February, about eleven o'clock in the morning, I was in my back parlour[3] adjoining the shop – the folding-doors between the shop and the parlour were open; I saw a boy run out – nobody was in the shop. I followed the boy, and as I ran through the shop I missed five silk handkerchiefs and one cotton one; he must have crept under the counter to the end of the window to take them – they could not have been reached without creeping under the counter; I had put them there that morning. I followed him into the street, crying Stop thief! and Rickman secured him. I saw him all the way up the street till he turned the corner. I am sure he is the boy; Rickman was pursuing the boy who ran out of the shop. He brought the prisoner back, and the handkerchiefs were found in his hat – they cost me 5 s. each.

TIMOTHY RICKMAN. I am constable[4] of St. Marylebone. I was standing in my shop, which is about thirty-six yards from Blakeman's, heard the cry of Stop thief! and ran out – the prisoner ran by my door. I pursued, and secured him about six yards off. I found the handkerchiefs in his hat.

(Property produced and sworn to.)

THOMAS BLAKEMAN. I am the prosecutrix's[5] son. I saw the handkerchiefs found in the prisoner's hat. I was down stairs when they were taken.

Prisoner's Defence. I heard the cry, and saw a little boy about my size going along; he dropped the handkerchiefs. I told him he had dropped them; he said, 'Never mind, keep them,' and I put them into my hat.

GUILTY. – DEATH. Aged 9.

Second Middlesex Jury, before Mr. Justice Richardson.

[1]indicted – charged with a crime

[2]haberdasher's shop – shop which sells small items for sewing and clothing

[3]parlour – a sitting room

[4]constable – someone paid to uphold the law and arrest criminals

[5]prosecutrix – a woman bringing a charge of crime against another person

Activity 2

Check your understanding of Source B opposite by answering the following questions.

a. Who are Timothy Rickman and Thomas Blakeman?

b. What is the shop owner's evidence for blaming Charles Elliott?

c. Who does Charles Elliott blame for the crime he is accused of?

Now consider the exam-style question below and how you should approach it.

You need to refer to **Source A** and **Source B** for this question.

Use details from *both* sources. Write a summary of the different ways the crimes affected the people involved. **[8 marks]**

Activity 3

a. Copy the question above and underline the key words.

b. Read Source A and Source B. To answer this question you must identify which of the people mentioned in the text may have been affected by the crimes.

Look at the lists of people below. With a partner, discuss how each one is affected by the crime that was committed and which you think offer the strongest points for use in your answer.

Source A	How is this character affected?	Source B	How is this character affected?
Delta airlines and people flying with them		The accused: Charles Elliot	
Twitter users		The shop owner: Martha Blakeman	
The boy's lawyer Ken Papenfus		The son of the shop owner	
SeaWorld theme park		The constable	
The White House			

The points you chose in Activity 3 for how each character is affected could be a useful way of organizing your answer to Question 2. You could write one paragraph about each of the three strongest points you have identified to create a three-paragraph answer. In each paragraph you should:

- make a statement about a clear difference between the two texts in line with what the question is asking

- select evidence from both texts relevant to the aspect you have identified

- explain the references/textual details you have chosen by answering the questions 'What's different?' and 'What can be inferred from this?'

Activity 4

Use a table like the one below to examine the different effects of the crime described. One example has been done for you. Copy and complete the table, choosing two more aspects of each text and using PEE.

Source A	Source B
Point 1: loss of money for SeaWorld	Point 1: crime affected the shop owner victim by potential loss of stock
Evidence:	Evidence: 'I missed five silk handkerchiefs and one cotton one'
Explanation: financial loss to a company	Explanation: material loss to the shop owner
Point 2:	Point 2:
Evidence:	Evidence:
Explanation:	Explanation:
Point 3:	Point 3:
Evidence:	Evidence:
Explanation:	Explanation:

Now look at a student's answer to Question 2 in exam conditions together with the teacher's comment.

Activity 5

Discuss with a partner how you could improve the marked student answer below to gain full marks. Then develop this student's answer in full, in accordance with the teacher's feedback. Use what you have learned in Activities 3 and 4.

Firstly in source A the criminal is affected by his crime by benefiting from the judge's sentence and despite 'causing chaos', the judge says to the boy 'you got carried away by the fact you thought you were cool', and that a serious sentence would 'destroy him'. The judge's words suggest that his crime shows that he is too young for serious punishment at 16, as it would do more harm than good. In source B however the criminal is affected by the crime because he is sentenced to death. This is shown by the final line 'GUILTY. – DEATH . Aged 9.' This is terrible and shocking and it seems very wrong that this could happen. It shows that the contexts of these texts were very different and that people's attitudes have changed a lot to do with crimes.

✓ Clear point of the effect of the crime

✓ Clearly linked to question

✓ Discourse marker for contrast

✓ Accurate point of difference

✓ Inference explored

✓ Relevant quotation. But where is your comment on it that shows inference?

✗ Not relevant. Your personal opinions are not asked for. You are just finding the differences shown in the texts and using inference to explain what they suggest.

Exam tip ✔

You don't have to understand every bit of a 19th-century text to be able to comment on language features used. It helps to look for the main clause in longer sentences, to establish 'who' is doing the action, and what that action is.

Teacher comments:

This is a sound start because you make a clear point about each text related to the question and establish a difference between them. You also use relevant quotations for each text and make an inference about Source A. Now extend this answer to include two more points about each text to establish their differences if you can. Establish the differences between each text in relation to the question, use quotation, and explore inference. Remember not to get carried away with your own opinions. This question is only asking you to look at what the texts suggest rather than give your personal judgements, even if you do feel strongly about what you have read.

Selecting clear and relevant textual details

When answering Question 2, it can be very easy to focus on one source text more than the other. You must refer to or select textual details evenly from *both* texts to support your answer. As the time and space you have to answer Question 2 is limited, make sure you pick the most relevant short references/textual details.

Try to integrate the quotations you select into your statements about the source texts. This can help you to focus on the most relevant part of the quotation.

Activity 6

Compare the two statements below and discuss them with a partner. How has one student created a more precise point using quotation?

Jack

The shop owner thinks that the boy in court is the thief: 'I am sure he is the boy'.

Helena

The shop owner is 'sure' that the boy in court is the thief.

Activity 7

Read the following statements about the article: 'Teenager who hacked governments worldwide is spared jail' on pages 146–147.

Which of the textual details offers the best short, relevant quotation to support each statement?

a. The judge is sympathetic that the boy did not realise the seriousness of his actions.

  i. 'District Judge Diane Baker said she was sparing him a custodial sentence as it would "destroy him"'.

  ii. "I think you got carried away by the fact you thought you were cool, you thought you were clever."

  iii. "I don't think there would be any positive outcome for you going into a youth detention centre."

b. The hacker was unaware of what he was doing and the potentially dangerous consequences.

  i. "I didn't really know how serious it was."

  ii. 'the boy described hacking as a hobby.'

  iii. 'Analysis of a laptop found at his address revealed conversations using Skype between him and another user'

When answering Question 2 in the exam, you can use discourse markers to organize your answer. These can help you to indicate the differences you have identified and the inferences you have made.

Activity 8

a. Copy out the list of discourse markers below.

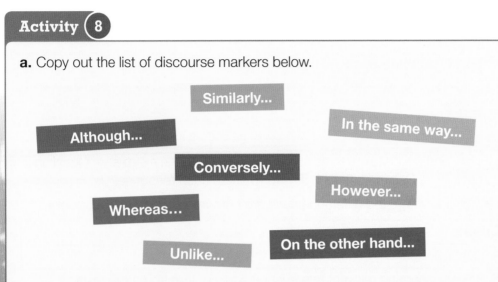

Similarly...

In the same way...

Although...

Conversely...

However...

Whereas...

On the other hand...

Unlike...

b. Write out the words in two columns headed *similarity* and *difference*.

- Decide which of the discourse markers can be used to identify difference.
- Decide which of the discourse markers can be used to identify similarity.

Check your answers are correct before learning these as part of your revision.

Exam tip ✔

When you are making inferences, remember to use the phrases below to make this clear. This will help the examiner see where you have used your skills of inference and credit you for this.

- We can assume that...
- This suggests...
- This shows...

Activity 9

Read the following exam-style question:

> You need to refer to **Source A** and **Source B** for this question:
>
> Use details from *both* sources. Write a summary of the differences between the lives of the two boys.

Choose *one* point you could make about the difference in the lives of the two criminals accused in Sources A and B in answer to this question.

Write a paragraph establishing that difference. In your paragraph you should:

- make a clear *statement* about the social backgrounds of each criminal
- use an appropriate discourse marker to establish the point of difference
- include relevant *references/textual details* from both texts
- make clear *inferences* from the selected evidence to support your statement.

Exam tip ✔

Remember you can quote single words, phrases or sentences from the source texts. The references/textual details must clearly support your statement and be relevant to the question focus. Short and sharp quotations tend to save time and encourage precision.

Exam tip ✔

In the exam you may encounter a text about a topic or time that you know something about. Remember this is a test of reading skills, so *only* include information stated or implied in the source texts, rather than your personal knowledge or opinions.

Synthesis and interpretation

In your answer to Question 2 you must show clear synthesis and interpretation of both texts and provide relevant evidence from both texts. Remember, to synthesize you need to:

- select and combine relevant information or ideas from both source texts
- make clear inferences
- justify your conclusions based on the references/textual details you have chosen.

Activity 10

a. Below and opposite are three student responses to the exam-style Question 2 in Activity 9. Use the criteria below to evaluate each response.

- Decide where the different criteria are demonstrated in each response.

Criteria
A Identifies clear differences between the texts
B Selects clear and relevant references/textual details from both texts
C Makes clear inferences from both texts
D Shows clear synthesis and interpretation of both texts, combining information to create a summary

- Rank the answers in order of quality: 1 for the strongest and 3 for the weakest. Write a paragraph to explain your reasons, using the sentence starters that follow.

> My ranking of the students is:
>
> _____ has written the strongest answer because...
>
> _____ has written the weakest answer because...

b. Did you notice where one student found a similarity but then refined it to show how they were different? This is skilful analysis. Write down which student does this and copy out the discourse marker used to establish difference.

Joshua

There are lots of differences about the effects of the crime. There are lots of views about this given in both texts as the judges think they have had an effect on people. The crimes are both committed by boys. Both of them have to go to court. These texts are written in different times and it shows that attitudes have changed. The boy Elliott might not have done the crime though whereas it is clear that the computer hacker did as he admitted to it.

Jamie

The texts shows how criminals are punished for their crimes and the negative effect that crimes have on their victims. The shopkeeper and her family are affected by Elliot's stealing. The woman and her son are angry about this and they report what happened to the court. Source B says 'He brought the prisoner back, and the handkerchiefs were found in his hat – they cost me 5 s. each' which shows that the boy caused a nuisance to people in the retail business and the police.

Kamil

> Both texts show that crime has an effect on victims and also the criminal themselves. Source A suggests that cyber crime and hacking is a serious offence and can effect the government, and foreign affairs. For example he 'shutdown government networks across the world and sent bomb threats'. This suggests that the crime could be believed to be a terror attack, which could have huge financial implications. Source B also lists details about financial cost to the victim who was a shop owner as she says 'they cost me 5 s. each'. However the difference here is that the costs are to an individual and are also relatively small, even though the sum mentioned would be of greater value in the nineteenth century.

Try it yourself

Activity 11

Complete the exam-style Question 2, previously looked at on page 153, using all the skills you have built so far.

> You need to refer to **Source A** and **Source B** for this question:
>
> Use details from *both* sources. Write a summary of the differences between the lives of the two boys.

Progress check

Now that you have practised the skills needed for Question 2, carry out the progress check below.

a. Look back at your answer to Activity 11. Annotate your answer to pick out the evidence that shows the following key skills:

Key Skills I can:	Confident I can do this.	OK Sometimes I can do this.	Not sure I need to practise this more.
make statements that show *clear* similarities between the texts			
make *clear* inferences from both texts			
demonstrate *clear* interpretations of both texts			
select *clear* references/textual details relevant to the focus of the question from both texts.			

b. Identify any improvements you would need to make to your original answer to meet the key skills given in the table above. Rewrite your response as necessary, highlighting the changes you have made.

3 Question 3

Understanding how a writer uses language

Assessment Objective

- Explain, comment on and analyse how writers use language to achieve effects and influence readers, using relevant subject terminology to support their views (AO2)

Question 3 is worth 12 marks and assesses your ability to analyse the effects of a writer's choices of language. You will need to show *clear understanding* of language by:

- *explaining clearly* the effects of the writer's choices of language
- selecting a range of *relevant* textual details
- making *clear and accurate* use of subject terminology.

The words in italics are the skills that mark out a stronger response from a weaker answer. In this section, you will explore exactly what is required for each skill when answering Question 3 as you work through this section.

In the exam this question could relate to either Source A *or* Source B. This means you might be analysing modern or 19th-century language. When you answer this question, remember to read the source text closely, looking carefully for the following:

- words and phrases chosen for effect
- language features, for example, metaphor, simile, and so on
- sentence forms and patterns.

In your response, you will need to explain the effects that these words and phrases, language features, and sentence forms and patterns create in relation to the focus of the question.

Exam tip ✔

This question could focus on a relatively short extract from one of the source texts. When you re-read the source text, read slowly and consider every detail and whether it uses interesting language.

Activity 1

Look back at what you must do in your response to Question 3 above. Write out the title 'Tips for answering Question 3'. Then write out the top *four* elements from the list below that *must* be included in a strong answer.

- Textual details, for example, quotations and examples
- Points about language that link to the exact focus of the question asked
- One quotation to support your answer
- Comments about the writer's life
- Language terminology, for example: noun, metaphor, short sentences
- Explanation of the effects of the language used
- Comments on the text's structure
- Comments about whether you like or dislike the text

Answering the question

To help organize your time, give yourself 1 minute per mark for each reading question, plus a little checking time. As Question 3 is worth 12 marks, you should spend approximately 12 minutes on your answer, plus 1 minute checking time.

Look at the following exam-style Question 3 referring to Source B, on page 158.

> You now need to refer to *Source B*, from **lines 1–16.**
>
> How does Dr Forbes use language to describe the mountain landscape?

Follow the steps below to make sure that your answer to Question 3 can meet all of the key skills required.

Exam tip ✔

Remember to read the set section of the source text carefully. Pay attention to every word, phrase and piece of punctuation and to the sentence structure. Think about how the language features you identify can help you to answer the question set.

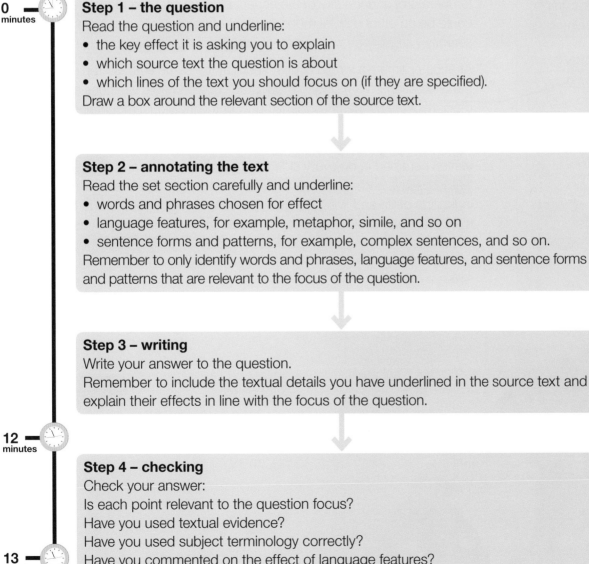

0 minutes

Step 1 – the question
Read the question and underline:
• the key effect it is asking you to explain
• which source text the question is about
• which lines of the text you should focus on (if they are specified).
Draw a box around the relevant section of the source text.

Step 2 – annotating the text
Read the set section carefully and underline:
• words and phrases chosen for effect
• language features, for example, metaphor, simile, and so on
• sentence forms and patterns, for example, complex sentences, and so on.
Remember to only identify words and phrases, language features, and sentence forms and patterns that are relevant to the focus of the question.

Step 3 – writing
Write your answer to the question.
Remember to include the textual details you have underlined in the source text and explain their effects in line with the focus of the question.

12 minutes

Step 4 – checking
Check your answer:
Is each point relevant to the question focus?
Have you used textual evidence?
Have you used subject terminology correctly?
Have you commented on the effect of language features?

13 minutes

One student has annotated Source B below, selecting words and phrases, language features, and sentence forms and patterns.

Look at the annotations. Some explain the effects created but others just identify language features.

Sibilance = to convey relaxing effect

Figurative language – metaphor = it is perfect

Semicolons linking several sentences together = the huge view of the world

Source B

Emotive language, using adjectives = perfection

Alliteration

Proper nouns = the scenery makes these elements come alive

Image – figurative language

"Sitting there, up in mid-heaven, as it were, on the smooth, warm ledge of our rock, in one of the sunniest noons of a summer day, amid air cooled by the elevation and the perfect exposure to the most delicious temperature; under a sky of the richest blue we seemed to feel as if there
5   could be no other mental mood but that of an exquisite[1] yet cheerful serenity[2], a luxurious perception of Beauty and Loveliness.

At another time – it would almost seem at the same time, so rapid was the alternation from mood to mood, the immeasurable vastness and majesty of the scene, the gigantic bulk of the individual mountains, the
10 peaks towering so far beyond the level of our daily earth, as to seem more belonging to the sky than to it, our own elevated and isolated station hemmed in on every side by untrodden wastes and impassable walls of snow, and, above all, the utter silence, and the absence of every indication of life and living things suggesting the thought that the foot of
15 man had never trodden, and never would tread there: these ideas would excite a tone of mind entirely different – solemn, awful, melancholy."

[1]exquisite – perfect

[2]serenity – calm

Set of three

Adjectives

Just as for Question 2 in Paper 1, you must explain the effect of the writer's choices of language in line with the focus you have been given. Every time that you identify a relevant word, phrase, language feature, sentence form or pattern, ask yourself the following questions:

- Why has the writer chosen this?
- What effect does this have on the reader in line with the question asked?
- In this question, how would it make readers understand the doctor's experience of the mountains? Why might you, as you read it, wish you could actually experience the place?

Activity 2

Look back at the annotations opposite. The student has not noted down the effect of alliteration, image – figurative language, adjectives or the set of three.

Copy and complete the notes about the effect of each language feature mentioned, to finish the list below.

> 'mood to mood, the immeasurable' – alliteration of 'm' =
>
> 'walls of snow' – image, figurative language =
>
> 'untrodden', 'impassable' – adjectives =
>
> 'solemn, awful, melancholy' – set of three =

Remember to link it to the question: How does Dr Forbes use language to describe the mountain landscape?

Read the explanation one student has written linked to their first annotation. They have used the PEE (point–evidence–explain) structure to organize this response.

> You now need to refer to *Source B*, from **lines 1–16**.
> How does Dr Forbes use language to describe the mountain landscape?

Fabio

Source B uses figurative language to describe the mountain landscape. One example is 'up in mid-heaven, as it were.' As well as giving information about the mountains being high, this metaphor makes the mountains seem holy and that the doctor feels as if he is with god. This helps the reader understand more than just how the mountains look: they can imagine how inspiring the landscape feels.

Point

Evidence

Explanation

Activity 3

a. Using the PEE structure on page 159, write a paragraph about the following quotation and related note on its effect.

> 'sunniest noons of a summer day' – sibilance = to convey relaxing effect

b. Now do the same for the next two annotations to explain the effects of the words and phrases, language features, and sentence forms and patterns identified. Remember your explanations should focus on how these make readers understand the experience of the mountains:

> 'exquisite… cheerful… luxurious' – emotive language, using adjectives = perfection

> 'Beauty' and 'Loveliness' – proper nouns = the scenery makes these elements come alive.

Read part of one student's answer below which focuses on the second section of this text (lines 7–16). It has been annotated to explain how it demonstrates features of a strong response.

Doug

Feature identified using correct terminology

Relevant textual detail

Examines effect on the reader

Clear explanation

Explains effect

In the second paragraph the doctor presents a description of the mountains which emphasizes the size and more difficult aspects of the place. For example he uses the image of 'walls of snow.' The word 'walls' suggests that they are fixed and difficult to pass and would help the reader imagine a very different place from their own home. He adds to this by using many adjectives that emphasize the huge strength of the place. For example 'immeasurable' and 'majesty' help the reader imagine a place where man is small and nature is both big in size and importance. To convey the size of the place he uses repeated semicolons to make the sentences build up and up, like the mountain ranges he is describing. This helps the reader understand how breathless the doctor feels in seeing the huge mountain area.

Range of language features mentioned

Subject terminology used clearly and accurately

Activity 4

a. In your response to Question 3, you need to select a range of relevant textual details. With a partner, decide where you think the student:

- chooses the shortest and most relevant quotation to support a point made
- weaves quotations and reference into his own sentences to explain the writer's use of language
- looks at punctuation or sentence structures in addition to words.

b. How could the student pinpoint where the semicolons are used, without copying out an extremely long quotation into his answer?

c. Add two further points about paragraph 2 (lines 7–16) of the source text and develop them into paragraphs to continue this answer at the same strong standard. Use the sentence starters below to begin your writing.

> Another technique that Dr Forbes uses...
>
> In addition, he...

Exam tip ✔

When answering Question 3 in the exam, think about the words and phrases you use to introduce each piece of analysis. This highlights that you know the *effect* of language; you are not just spotting features. Sentence starters you should learn include:

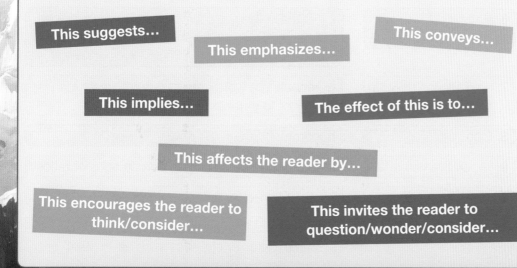

This suggests...

This emphasizes...

This conveys...

This implies...

The effect of this is to...

This affects the reader by...

This encourages the reader to think/consider...

This invites the reader to question/wonder/consider...

Clear and accurate subject terminology

In your answer to Question 3, you need to make clear and accurate use of subject terminology in your response. Think about the focus of the question and link the references you make to different language features with the effects these create.

Exam tip ✔

Make sure you have learned the full list of terms before your final exam. You should be able to recognize their use in a text. Remember to comment on their effect in relation to the focus of the question you are answering.

Activity 5

a. Look at the list below of some of the language features that you might find in a non-fiction text. Some of these you might also find in Paper 1 fiction source texts. Turn back to page 87 to remind yourself of the language features you have already studied to analyse fiction texts.

b. Link each term to its definition below, for example: 1 = b

Terms	Definitions
1. hyperbole	**a.** a number of connected items or names written consecutively
2. figurative language (simile, metaphor, personification)	**b.** exaggeration
3. facts	**c.** viewpoints of other people that may or may not be factually true
4. familiar references, anecdotes	**d.** a question asked for dramatic effect and not intended to get an answer
5. evidence from others	**e.** the formality or informality of a written or spoken style
6. statistics	**f.** imaginative language that is used to convey an idea. Includes simile, metaphor and personification. It should not be read literally. For example, 'walls of snow'
7. opinions	**g.** repeating a word or phrase to make an idea clearer or to emphasize its importance
8. tone	**h.** commands, e.g. 'Sit down', 'Never do that'
9. imperative verbs	**i.** data or numbers such as percentages or ratios
10. the second person	**j.** use of 'I'/'we'
11. the first person	**k.** statements that are provable and true. For example, dates or statistics such as 'in 1984' or '70% of people interviewed said…'
12. formal or informal register	**l.** using three examples or points together for extra power and emphasis
13. colloquial language	**m.** quotations, reported speech or references to experts on the topic

14. list	**n.** personal stories or references to things that are well-known to the reader/audience
15. rhetorical question	**o.** the language of everyday conversation rather than formal language
16. repetition	**p.** use of 'you' to address the reader or listener
17. power of three	**q.** words that show the writer's attitude, for example, humorous or sarcastic

Try it yourself

The following extract is taken from a series of newspaper articles called 'The day I made a difference'. Contributors write about how they give something positive to their society.

Source A

The day I made a difference

Homeless youngsters need a chat with a mum. My home is open to them

by Jo Randle, Nightstop volunteer

Some young people don't have the benefit of a restful, supportive family home, or a chat with their mum, so that's what I offer them for a couple of nights

5 I was driving home from work one evening when I heard an advert for Nightstop South Yorkshire on the radio. I had never heard of it before, but immediately I thought: 'I could do that.'

When you host with Nightstop, you agree to
10 have a young person facing homelessness come to stay in your house for a night or two.

The first time I hosted it was a young man, but I've always been someone who takes things as they come, so I wasn't worried about opening
15 up my home. When I open the door and meet someone who's going to be staying with me, the main thing I'm thinking about is usually what's in the fridge and whether they'll like what I'm cooking that night.

My first guest was very well spoken and had 20
been to university – he wasn't at all what you would expect of a young person experiencing homelessness. Often these young people have been asked to leave the family home for one reason or another. I've had people kicked out on 25
to the streets when they have come out as gay, people with learning difficulties whose carers can't cope, people whose family life was just too unstable for them to stay.

That first evening my son came round to make 30
sure everything was okay – he's pretty used to my madcap ideas though and doesn't bother doing that any more. The last I heard my first guest had found a job and was looking for a private tenancy. 35

I suffered a bereavement[1] a few years ago and it could so easily have been me in a similarly difficult situation. We don't know what is around the corner, what will happen to us or how we will react. People often seem to think homeless people are all dirty, with substance abuse problems, and that it's their fault they are where they are. But that just isn't the case. I have had people from all walks of life come through my front door.

A few months ago I hosted a young man who really tugged on my heartstrings. He'd had a tough family life, things had come to a head and he had been asked to leave by his mum. He wasn't a bad lad, he just needed some stability.

Once, when we were chatting, he said to me: 'I've never done this.' I asked what he meant, and he said that he'd never been able to just sit down and have a chat with his mum. It's little things like that we take for granted – some young people don't have the luxury of a restful and supportive family home, so that's what I try to offer them for a couple of nights.

I'm not some amazing, charitable, selfless person, but I live alone in a large house with spare bedrooms. I have the ability to do this, so I should. I considered becoming a foster carer in the past, but the commitment was just too much – Nightstop is flexible and I can host around my existing plans, like helping out with the grandchildren.

Luckily, I know that most of the young people I've hosted so far are now in some kind of secure and permanent accommodation – some have their own tenancies. I'm not inviting someone with the problems of entrenched[2] street homelessness into my home – I'm helping to prevent those problems from ever taking root, by providing safe accommodation while the other services available to these young people kick in. I always had a house full of kids when my children were younger and not much fazes me, so hosting these kids who've fallen on hard times is my way of feeling like I'm doing something to help.

[1]bereavement – losing a close relative or friend through death

[2]entrenched – established habit that is difficult to change

Look at the following exam-style Question 3 about 'The day I made a difference', and complete Activity 6 below.

You now need to refer *only* to Source A from **lines 20 to 45.**

How does the writer use language to describe the homeless people she works with?

Activity 6

a. Underline the key words in the question.

b. Re-read the source text on pages 163–164. Select some relevant words and phrases, language features, and sentence forms and patterns that will help you to answer the question.

c. Add the relevant subject terminology to identify any features you have chosen.

d. Now write a full exam response to this question.

Progress check

Now that you have practised the skills needed for Question 3, carry out the progress check below.

a. Look back at your answer in Activity 6. Annotate your answer to pick out the evidence that shows the following key skills:

Key Skills I can:	Confident I can do this.	OK Sometimes I can do this.	Not sure I need to practise this more.
show *clear* understanding when I *explain clearly* the effects of the writer's choices of language			
use subject terminology *clearly and accurately* when writing about language			
select a *range* of *relevant* textual details.			

b. Look at your annotated answer. If it is missing, or has very little, of one type of annotation, review your work and try to improve it to meet the key skill requirements. You could work with a partner to help each other identify how you could improve.

4 Question 4

Assessment Objective

- Compare writers' ideas and perspectives, as well as how these are conveyed, across two or more texts (AO3)

Comparing writers' ideas and perspectives

Question 4 is worth 16 marks. It assesses your ability to compare *the whole* of both texts, focusing on the writers' ideas and perspectives and how they are conveyed. You will need to:

- show a *clear understanding* of the different ideas and perspectives in both sources
- compare ideas and perspectives in *a clear and relevant way*
- select *relevant supporting detail* from both texts
- *explain clearly* how writers' methods are used and the effects they create.

Question 4 brings together all the skills you have used separately to answer the earlier questions.

Exam tip ✔

Compare means that you must consider similarities and differences.

Activity 1

Question 4 might ask you to compare how writers convey their:

- ideas or attitudes
- viewpoints or perspectives
- experiences.

Link each word or phrase in the left-hand column to its definition in the right-hand column. Remember to think about what each phrase means in the context of answering Question 4.

Question focus	Definition
A. Writer's ideas or attitudes	**1.** A point of view on a particular topic, for example, in support of, or against
B. Writer's viewpoint or perspective	**2.** Things that have happened to the writer that might affect them, teach them or change their attitudes
C. Writer's experience	**3.** Specific thoughts a writer has about a topic and suggestions they make

How to tackle Question 4 in the exam

1. This question focuses on comparison of two texts written at different historical times.

Read each text and identify the:

Purpose

Audience

Text type

You must be clear about:

- when each text was written,

- how the writer's attitudes might relate to the views of the time.

2. Underline the key words in the question.

3. Identify textual evidence which supports the focus of the question – line references (useful when discussing structure) and quotations (useful when discussing language).

4. Explain the writer's methods used in your examples.

Read the source text on pages 168–169. This is adapted from an essay 'Going to see a man hanged' by the writer William Makepeace Thackeray, written in 1840. The extract describes the festivities associated with the public hanging of François Benjamin Courvoisier, a servant who murdered his master.

Activity 2

a. As you read, ask yourself the following questions:

- What is the opinion expressed about the event of a public hanging?

- Where is the evidence for this?

Write down an example of a shift or change in the writing. This can often help you identify changes in structure, language and therefore tone.

b. Discuss your ideas with a partner.

Source A

'Going to see a man hanged' by William Makepeace Thackeray, July 1840

The crowd has grown very dense by this time. It is about six o'clock, and there is great heaving, and pushing, and swaying to and fro. The character of the crowd was as yet, however, quite festive. Jokes
5 bandying[1] about here and there, and jolly laughs breaking out.

Really the time passed away with extraordinary quickness. A thousand things of the sort related here came to amuse us. First the workmen knocking and
10 hammering at the scaffold, mysterious clattering of blows was heard within it, and a ladder painted black was carried round, and into the interior of the edifice[2] by a small side door. We all looked at this little ladder and at each other — things began to be very interesting.

It was past seven now; the quarters[3] rang and passed away; the crowd began to grow very eager and more quiet, and we turned back every now and then and looked at St. Sepulchre's[4] clock.
15 Half-an-hour, twenty-five minutes. What is he doing now? He has his irons[5] off by this time. A quarter: he's in the press-room[6] now, no doubt. Now at last we had come to think about the man we were going to see hanged. How slowly the clock crept over the last quarter! Those who were able to turn round and see (for the crowd was now extraordinarily dense) chronicled the time, eight minutes, five minutes; at last — ding, dong, dong, dong! — the bell is tolling the chimes of eight.

* *

20 Between the writing of this line and the last, the pen has been put down, as the reader may suppose, and the person who is addressing him has gone through a pause of no very pleasant thoughts and recollections. The whole of the sickening, ghastly, wicked scene passes before the eyes again; and, indeed, it is an awful one to see, and very hard and painful to describe.

As the clock began to strike, an immense sway and movement swept over the whole of that vast
25 dense crowd. They were all uncovered directly, and a great murmur arose, more awful, bizarre, and indescribable than any sound I had ever before heard. Women and children began to shriek horribly.

Just then, from under the black prison-door, a pale quiet head peered out. It was shockingly bright and distinct; it rose up directly, and a man in black appeared on the scaffold, and was silently followed by about four more dark figures. The first was a tall grave man: we all knew who the second
30 man was. 'That's he — that's he!' you heard the people say.

Courvoisier bore his punishment like a man, and walked very firmly. He was dressed in a new black suit, as it seemed: his shirt was open. His arms were tied in front of him. He opened his hands in a helpless kind of way, and clasped them once or twice together. He turned his head here and there, and looked about him for an instant with a wild imploring[7] look. His mouth was contracted into a
35 sort of pitiful smile. He went and placed himself at once under the beam, with his face towards St. Sepulchre's. The tall grave man in black twisted him round swiftly in the other direction, and, drawing from his pocket a night-cap, pulled it tight over the patient's head and face. I am not

ashamed to say that I could look no more, but shut my eyes as the last dreadful act was going on which sent
40 this wretched guilty soul into the presence of God.

The Great Moral Lesson at Horsemonger Lane Gaol, Nov. 13.

[1]bandying – casually passing around

[2]edifice – a large structure

[3]the quarters – the bells that ring every fifteen minutes

[4]St. Sepulchre's – the church next to Newgate prison in London

[5]irons – shackles or restrains for wrists and ankles

[6]press-room – the place where leg irons were removed

[7]imploring – pleading, begging

Activity 3

Copy out the table below and use it to analyse the text. Refer to the list of writers' methods on page 162 to help you complete it.

POINT	EVIDENCE		EXPLANATION
Define the writer's views and attitudes to the hanging event. Is there any shift or change in his views and attitudes in the extract?	Relevant quotations	Define the writer's methods in the quotations	Analyse the effect on the reader
1. At the beginning, he (and the crowd) are interested by the event's preparations.	'things began to be very interesting'	The adjectival phrase 'very interesting' emphasizes his opinion that the scene is fascinating and comments on the actions of the workers at the hanging.	Original readers may have agreed with Thackeray as many went to watch hangings. It helps the reader share his experience of this event with the details of the crowd and workers.
2. He shares in the excitement of the crowd.			
3. There is a shift at line 20 where he reflects as he writes about the experience.			
4. He realizes he feels horror about watching a hanging.			

Now read an extract from the autobiography of the youngest member of a family of English executioners, Albert Pierrepoint. Henry Pierrepoint, his brother Thomas, and his son Albert hanged some of the most notorious criminals of the 20th century, and prided themselves in their skill. Here, Albert describes the first hanging where he was in charge.

Activity 4

As you read, ask yourself the following questions about the text:

- What is the opinion expressed about hanging?
- How has the writer chosen to convey his perspective about the event of hanging?
- How does the writer structure his writing to achieve this?
- What language does the writer choose to achieve this?
- How does the tone of the writing reflect this?

The first paragraph of the text has been annotated with some comments in response to these questions to support your thinking.

IMPORTANT. Negative emphasizes it is unusual.

SIGNIFICANT PERSONALLY. Temporal connective emphasizes his new experience.

KIND. Adjective shows he wants to reduce suffering of the criminal.

Source B

Extract from *Executioner: Pierrepoint* by Albert Pierrepoint

This could not be an ordinary occasion for me, however successfully I acted as if it was just routine. For the first time I was looking at a man who was to die at my hands, studying him technically, but only to calculate how to be most merciful to him. I was interested in his physique, which affected

5   my calculation of the drop I should give, and in his temperament and behaviour which would give me an indication of how I could expect him to act next morning.

I looked around the green-painted execution chamber to check that everything was in order. I picked up a stray thread of twine from where it

10   has fallen on the traps. With a piece of chalk I re-lined the T-mark under the noose on the front drop where the prisoner's toes were to be aligned, the arches of the feet directly over the crack in the doors. I slightly shifted the cross-planks on either side of the T, and I made one final adjustment. I crossed to the lever and released a split pin that held the cotter pin fast,

15   and I eased out the cotter pin for half its length, so that, while still resisting an untimely push, the end of it was flush with the side of the lever. In action, even the time it took to withdraw an extra half-inch was important to me.

'Right', I said. 'Breakfast.' And we went away for bacon and eggs.

***

The prisoner was standing, facing me, smiling. I quickly strapped his wrists

20   and said, 'Follow me.'

The door in the side wall of the cell had been opened as I came in, and I walked through it into the execution chamber. He followed me, walking seven paces with the noose straight ahead of him, and the escorting officers mounting the cross planks gently stopped him as he stood on the T.

25 I had turned in time to face him. Eye to eye, that last look. Wade was stooping behind him, swiftly fastening the ankle strap. I pulled from my breast pocket the white cap, folded as carefully as a parachute, and drew it down over his head. 'Cheerio,' he said. I reached for the noose, pulled it down over the cap, tightened it to my right, pulled a rubber washer along

30 the rope to hold it, and darted to my left, crouching towards the cotter pin at the base of the lever. I was in the position of a sprinter at the start of a race as I went over the cross-plank, pulled the pin with one hand, and pushed the lever with the other, instinctively looking back as I did so. There was a snap as the falling doors were bitten and held by the rubber clips,

35 and the rope stood straight and still. The broken twine spooned down in a falling leaf, passed through a little eddy of dust, and floated into the pit.

We all left the execution chamber. Soon the Governor sent for me. 'I have seen your uncle work on many occasions,' he said. He is a very good man indeed. Never has he been any quicker than you have been this morning.'

40 Then I went below, and Wade lowered the rope. A dead man, being taken down from execution, is a uniquely broken body whether he is a criminal or Christ, and I received this flesh, leaning helplessly into my arms, with the linen round the loins, gentle with the reverence I thought due to the shell of any man who has sinned and suffered.

Before you begin to answer Question 4 in the exam, it can be helpful to identify the text type, audience and purpose of each text. You can use the acronym 'PAT' to help you remember this:

Purpose: for example, to inform, persuade, argue, entertain or a combination of these purposes

Audience: the intended reader or audience, for example, modern parents, educated adults in the late 19th century or today's teenagers

Text type: for example, a letter, speech, magazine or newspaper article

Activity 5

Identify the Purpose, Audience and Text type of Source B.

Exam tip ✔

Remember that in your final exam you will not have the time to make such detailed annotations, but you might find it helpful to underline key quotations and add single word annotations to identify specific methods.

Read the following exam-style Question 4.

> For this question, you need to refer to the **whole of Source A** together with the **whole of Source B**.
>
> Compare how the writers convey their different views on the event of a hanging.
>
> In your answer, you could:
> - compare their different views and perspectives
> - compare the methods they use to convey those views and experiences
> - support your ideas with quotations from both texts.

Look at the annotations below by a student. They are a strong example of identifying views conveyed about the hanging event at the end of Source B.

He considers every hanged man an individual

He suggests he has some sympathy for the hanged body – adjective

He thinks the executed man's body is empty – figurative language

> Then I went below, and Wade lowered the rope. A dead man, being taken down from execution, is a uniquely broken body whether he is a criminal or Christ, and I received this flesh, leaning helplessly into my arms, with the linen round the loins, gentle with the reverence I thought due to the shell of any man who has sinned and suffered.

He suggests that his role in the execution is almost moral and religious – religious language and references

Activity 6

Follow this model to annotate Source A (pages 168-169) and Source B (pages 170-171) in line with the exam-style Question 4 above. You could use the questions below to guide the annotations you make.

- What is the opinion expressed about the hanging event?
- How has the writer chosen to convey his view about the hanging event?
- How does the writer structure the writing to achieve this?
- What language does the writer choose to achieve this?
- How does the tone of the writing reflect this?

Tip ✔

Remind yourself of some useful discourse markers by looking back at page 153.

Activity 7

a. Copy and complete the table below to identify and compare the writers' different views on hanging and the details that suggest these. The left-hand column of the table suggests how you could structure your answer to the question.

b. Identify which points highlight a similarity between the attitudes in the two texts. Identify which points highlight a difference between the attitudes in the two texts.

Structure of your answer	Source A (Thackeray)	Source B (Pierrepoint)
Paragraph 1 of your answer	Point: the event of a hanging is *exciting* for the crowd and the writer Evidence: 'jolly laughs breaking out'	Point: the event of the first hanging is *significant* and important for the hangman Evidence: 'could not be an ordinary occasion'
Paragraph 2 of your answer	Point: the event of a hanging is *interesting* to watch in terms of staff and equipment Evidence: 'things began to be very interesting'	Point: the event and details of a hanging are *interesting* for the hangman (and his readers) because of the skills and equipment involved Evidence: 'noose…cross-planks…cotter pin'
Paragraph 3 of your answer	Point: The event of a hanging is a *social event* Evidence:	Point: the event of a hanging is a *professional event* – a job Evidence:
Paragraph 4 of your answer	Point: The event of a hanging is *unsettling* Evidence:	Point: The event of a hanging is *unsettling* Evidence:
Paragraph 5 of your answer	Point: The event of a hanging is *horrific* Evidence:	Point: the event of a hanging is *respectful and dignified* Evidence:

Activity 8

Write an answer for the exam-style Question 4 on page 172 by using the following paragraph structure:

Point on Source A

⬇

Evidence

⬇

Explanation

⬇

Point of similarity with or difference from Source B, linked by a discourse marker

⬇

Evidence

⬇

Explanation

Try it yourself

Activity 9

Read Source A and Source B on pages 174–176 and answer the exam-style Question 4 below.

For this question, you need to refer to the **whole of Source A** together with the **whole of Source B.**

Compare how the writers have conveyed their attitudes towards the people in need. In your answer, you could:

- compare their different views and descriptions
- compare the methods they use to convey those views and descriptions
- support your ideas with quotations from both texts.

Plan and then write your answer to the question. In the exam you will be given up to four pages to write your response. Use the planning structure on page 169 of this book and the paragraph structure given on page 173 to write each section.

Exam tip ✔

Remember to write about both texts equally. It's very easy when you are under pressure to get carried away and write about one of the texts while ignoring the other.

Source A is taken from a series of newspaper articles called 'The day I made a difference'. Contributors write about how they give something positive to their society.

Source A

The day I made a difference
Homeless youngsters need a chat with a mum. My home is open to them

by Jo Randle, Nightstop volunteer

Some young people don't have the benefit of a restful, supportive family home, or a chat with their mum, so that's what I offer them for a couple of nights

5   I was driving home from work one evening when I heard an advert for Nightstop South Yorkshire on the radio. I had never heard of it before, but immediately I thought: 'I could do that.'

When you host with Nightstop, you agree to
10   have a young person facing homelessness come to stay in your house for a night or two.

The first time I hosted it was a young man, but I've always been someone who takes things as they come, so I wasn't worried about opening up my home. When I open the door and meet someone   15 who's going to be staying with me, the main thing I'm thinking about is usually what's in the fridge and whether they'll like what I'm cooking that night.

My first guest was very well spoken and had been to university – he wasn't at all what you   20 would expect of a young person experiencing homelessness. Often these young people have been asked to leave the family home for one reason or another. I've had people kicked out on to the streets when they have come out as gay, people with learning difficulties whose carers can't cope, people whose family life was just too unstable for them to stay.

That first evening my son came round to make sure everything was okay – he's pretty used to my madcap ideas though and doesn't bother doing that any more. The last I heard my first guest had found a job and was looking for a private tenancy.

I suffered a bereavement[1] a few years ago and it could so easily have been me in a similarly difficult situation. We don't know what is around the corner, what will happen to us or how we will react. People often seem to think homeless people are all dirty, with substance abuse problems, and that it's their fault they are where they are. But that just isn't the case. I have had people from all walks of life come through my front door.

A few months ago I hosted a young man who really tugged on my heartstrings. He'd had a tough family life, things had come to a head and he had been asked to leave by his mum. He wasn't a bad lad, he just needed some stability.

Once, when we were chatting, he said to me: 'I've never done this.' I asked what he meant, and he said that he'd never been able to just sit down and have a chat with his mum. It's

little things like that we take for granted – some young people don't have the luxury of a restful and supportive family home, so that's what I try to offer them for a couple of nights.

I'm not some amazing, charitable, selfless person, but I live alone in a large house with spare bedrooms. I have the ability to do this, so I should. I considered becoming a foster carer in the past, but the commitment was just too much – Nightstop is flexible and I can host around my existing plans, like helping out with the grandchildren.

Luckily I know that most of the young people I've hosted so far are now in some kind of secure and permanent accommodation – some have their own tenancies. I'm not inviting someone with the problems of entrenched[2] street homelessness into my home – I'm helping to prevent those problems from ever taking root, by providing safe accommodation while the other services available to these young people kick in. I always had a house full of kids when my children were younger and not much fazes me, so hosting these kids who've fallen on hard times is my way of feeling like I'm doing something to help.

[1]bereavement – losing a close relative or friend through death

[2]entrenched – established habit that is difficult to change

Source B is an extract from the diary of an amateur artist who lived in London in 1864. In this extract he describes the beggars he encounters in St James's Park.

Source B

Extract from the diary of Arthur Munby

Friday, 15 July

Walking through St. James's Park about 4 p.m., I found the open spaces of sward[1] on either side the path thickly dotted over with strange dark objects. They were human beings; ragged men & ragged women; lying prone & motionless, not as those who lie down for rest & enjoyment, but
5   as creatures worn out and listless. A park keeper came up: who are these? I asked. They are men out of work, said he, and unfortunate girls; servant girls, many of them, what has been out of place and took to the streets, till they've sunk so low that they can't get a living. It's like this every day, till winter comes; and then what they do I don't know. They come as soon
10   as the gates opens; always the same faces: they bring broken victuals with 'em, or else goes to the soup kitchen in Vinegar Yard; and except for that, they lie about here all day. It's a disgrace Sir (said he), to go on in a City like this; and foreigners to see it, too! Why Sir, these unfortunates are all over the place: the ground (he added with a gesture of disgust) is lousy
15   with them'. I looked and still they did not move. The men were more or less tattered, but their dress was working dress, & so did not seem out of place. But the girls were clothed in what had once been finery: filthy draggled muslins[2]; thin remnants of shawls, all rent and gaping; crushed and greasy bonnets of fashionable shape, with sprigs of torn flowers, bits
20   of faded velvet, hanging from them. Their hands and faces were dirty & weather-stained; and they lay, not (as far as I saw) herding with the men, but singly or in little groups; sprawling about the grass in attitudes ungainly, and unfeminine, and bestial: one flat on her face, another curled up like a dog with her head between her knees; another with her knees bent
25   under her, and her cheek on the ground, and her arms spread out stiff and awkward, on either side of her. Every pose expressed an absolute degradation and despair: and the silence & deadness of the prostrate[3] crowd was appalling. I counted these as I went along; and on one side only of one path (leading from the lake to the Mall), there were one hundred
30   and five of them. 105 forlorn and foetid[4] outcasts – women, many of them – grovelling on the sward, in the bright sunshine of a July afternoon, with Carlton House Terrace and Westminster Abbey looking down at them, and infinite well-drest[5] citizens passing by on the other side.

[1]sward – lawn

[2]muslins – cotton dresses

[3]prostrate – lying down

[4]foetid – foul-smelling

[5]well-drest – well-dressed

EARLY MORNING.—THE ENUMERATOR TAKING THE CENSUS IN ST. JAMES'S PARK.

Progress check

Now that you have practised the skills needed for Question 4, carry out the progress check below.

a. Use three highlighter pens of different colours to highlight passages of your answer in Activity 9 to show where you have satisfied each of the key skills below.

Key Skills I can:	Confident I can do this.	OK Sometimes I can do this.	Not sure I need to practise this more.
compare ideas and perspectives in a *clear* and *relevant* way			
show a *clear* understanding of the different ideas and perspectives in both texts			
explain clearly how writers' methods are used			
select *relevant* detail to support my ideas from both texts.			

b. If any of your points do not match these skills, go back to your answer and make changes.

6 Paper 2 Section B: Writing

Section B, the Writing section of Paper 2 is worth 40 marks, the same as the Reading section. You should expect to spend about 45 minutes on your writing, with three stages to follow:

- planning (5–10 minutes)
- writing (30–35 minutes)
- checking, proofreading and making final improvements (5 minutes).

You will be given one writing task. It will be linked in a general way to the topic of the two source texts read in Section A. You can draw ideas or even occasional words and phrases from the source texts if you find them useful, but you do not have to. You must not copy out complete sentences or sections.

The task will ask you to express your own views about a topic, using Standard English. You will be given a specific purpose, audience and form for your writing (for example, an article for a school magazine).

It is crucial that you leave enough time for the Writing section because it is worth half your marks on this paper. Your teacher may advise you to start with the writing activity if you have a history of not leaving enough time to complete this section.

Understanding how your answers are marked

Your writing will be marked against two Assessment Objectives (AOs) in the Writing section of Paper 2:

Assessment Objective	The writing skills that you need to demonstrate
AO5 (Content and organization)	Communicate clearly, effectively and imaginatively, selecting and adapting tone, style and register for different forms, purposes and audiences. Organize information and ideas, using structural and grammatical features to support **coherence and cohesion** of texts.
AO6 (Technical accuracy)	Use a range of vocabulary and sentence structures for clarity, purpose and effect, with accurate spelling and punctuation.

> **Key term**
>
> **coherence and cohesion:** the way a piece of writing links together in terms of vocabulary, phrases, clauses, sentences and paragraphs

The writing question in Paper 2 is worth a maximum of 40 marks:

●　24 marks are available for content and organization (AO5)

●　16 marks are available for technical accuracy (AO6).

What is content and organization?

To gain good marks for content and organization you need to:

●　get your ideas across to the reader clearly

●　match your writing to whatever purpose, audience and form you have been given.

You will need to make deliberate choices of language and textual features, so that your writing affects your readers in the most powerful way possible. To assess this, the examiner will look at:

●　the way you use individual words and phrases

●　the way you sequence, link and present your points

●　the organization of your whole piece of writing, and the paragraphs and sections within it.

What is technical accuracy?

Technical accuracy is using words, punctuation and grammar correctly. Your written response needs to show that you can:

●　use a range of vocabulary

●　spell correctly, including more complex and ambitious words

●　write in correctly punctuated sentences

●　use a variety of sentence forms to achieve specific effects

●　write in Standard English.

Look at the skills above, alongside evidence of your work in the last year. Look back at past mock results and any other assessments you have done. What do teacher marking and feedback suggest you need to prioritize from this list? You should know more generally whether you need to prioritize:

●　reading skills

●　writing skills

●　exam technique

●　more than one of these.

1 Writing to present a viewpoint

Assessment Objectives

- Communicate clearly, effectively and imaginatively, selecting and adapting tone, style and register for different forms, purposes and audiences (AO5)

- Organize information and ideas, using structural and grammatical features to support coherence and cohesion of texts (AO5)

- Use a range of vocabulary and sentence structures for clarity, purpose and effect, with accurate spelling and punctuation (AO6)

The writing task

In Section B of Paper 2, the writing task is likely to present you with:

- an **assertion** such as 'Young people today care only for themselves and not for the good of society'

  and/or

- a statement of opinion, for example, 'The government's decision to force students to take traditional GCSE subjects rather than practical subjects is wrong. It ignores the range of young people in our schools and the skills society needs.'

You will then be asked to write a non-fiction text such as an article or letter for a particular publication, either supporting or arguing against the assertion or statement. Any audience named by the question will usually mean that you can write formally, for a general reader, rather than having to know about a specific person and their interests. This means that you must use Standard English with correct grammar, punctuation and spelling.

Look at the following exam-style writing task.

'For today's busy families, finding time to schedule exercise for children is a luxury not a necessity. Schools should take responsibility for this, not parents.'

Write a letter to the local MP who made this statement, in which you explain your response to her opinion.

Activity 1

Look carefully at the second part of the above writing task and identify the purpose, audience and text type/form for your writing.

Purpose: Choose from the terms below.

to inform	to argue	to persuade
to entertain	to describe	to instruct
to explain		

Audience:

Text type:

Planning your writing

Choosing your viewpoint

The title of Paper 2 is 'Writers' viewpoints and perspectives'. In the Writing section that writer is you! So you *must* have a **viewpoint** or adopt one for the task you have been given. You must establish your view on the topic given in the writing task, before you plan and write your response.

Activity 2

a. Read the statements below. For each one, highlight the key words that you need to consider when forming your own point of view on the topic. The first one is done for you.

i. 'The government's decision to force students to take traditional GCSE subjects rather than practical subjects is wrong. It ignores the range of young people in our schools and the skills society needs.'

ii. 'Animal testing can never be justified.'

iii. 'A vegetarian diet is the only humane and healthy diet. We should all follow this because eating meat is murder.'

iv. 'The standard of manners in this country is awful. It is time parents and schools taught young people how to act with consideration and politeness.'

v. 'Public libraries are a thing of the past. They are an unnecessary public expense in modern society.'

vi. 'Reality TV shows are a negative influence on today's youth. They emphasize show and celebrity over hard work and real talent.'

vii. 'Homelessness is increasing. These people are often in this situation because of terrible life experiences which are not their fault. It is our responsibility to support them to rebuild their lives.'

b. Plot your own viewpoint in response to each statement using a line like this:

Strongly disagree				Neutral				Strongly agree
1	2	3	4	5	6	7	8	9	10

Remember that you will need to give reasons to support your point of view.

Planning ideas

Once you have decided on your viewpoint, you need to identify the ideas you will present to support your point of view. Depending on your viewpoint, you might want to use one of the following planning structures to develop your ideas as you plan:

1. **Strongly agree** – all points of argument support the statement.

2. **Both agree and disagree:**

   a. More agree than disagree – most points of argument support the statement. A few points disagree with the statement.

   b. More disagree than agree – most points of argument disagree with the statement.

3. **Strongly disagree** – all points of argument disagree with the statement.

Exam tip ✔

You must keep returning to the key words of the question. Agreeing with the statement here is not the same as agreeing with the principle of public libraries (see page 183). The statement is against public libraries. Agreeing with the statement is arguing against public funding of public libraries.

Activity 3

a. Discuss the question below with a partner or your class. List some of the programmes you know that are linked to the category of 'reality TV'.

b. Choose the structure above that most closely reflects your own response to the following statement:

> 'Reality TV shows are a negative influence on today's youth.
> They emphasize show and celebrity over hard work and real talent.'

c. Use the planning format from Activity 2 to note down ideas to support your viewpoint. Outline some of your points – either agreeing, disagreeing, or a mix of both. Think carefully about any particular phrases or key words that you agree or disagree with.

Nadiya has started to plan a response to the following writing question, circling the key words in the statement and drafting her ideas on page 183:

> 'Public libraries are a thing of the past. They are an unnecessary public expense in modern society.'

> Write an article for a magazine in which you are either supporting or disagreeing with this view.

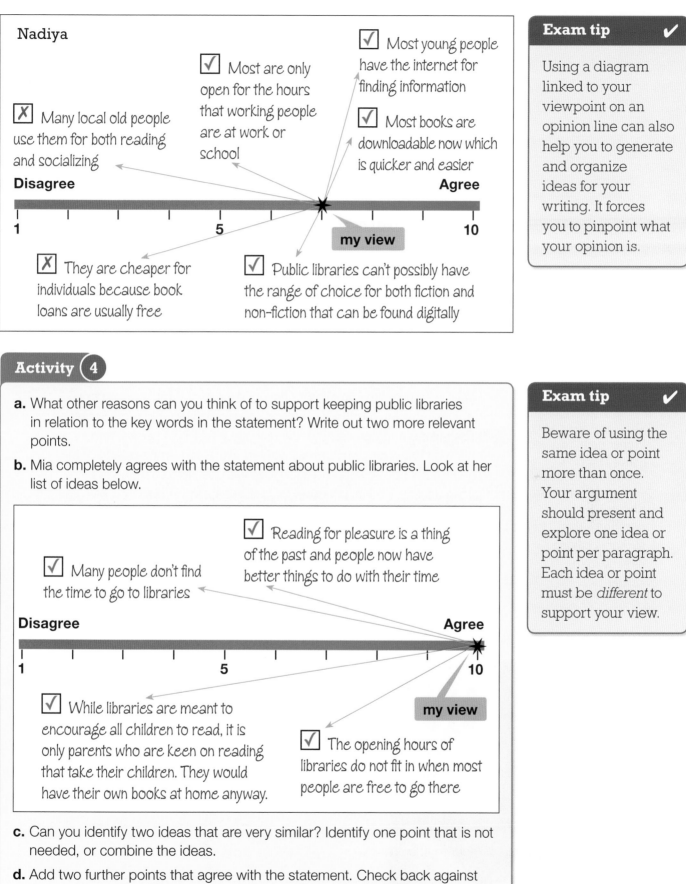

Nadiya

☒ Many local old people use them for both reading and socializing

☑ Most are only open for the hours that working people are at work or school

☑ Most young people have the internet for finding information

☑ Most books are downloadable now which is quicker and easier

Disagree   **Agree**

1   5   10

my view

☒ They are cheaper for individuals because book loans are usually free

☑ Public libraries can't possibly have the range of choice for both fiction and non-fiction that can be found digitally

Exam tip ✔

Using a diagram linked to your viewpoint on an opinion line can also help you to generate and organize ideas for your writing. It forces you to pinpoint what your opinion is.

Activity 4

a. What other reasons can you think of to support keeping public libraries in relation to the key words in the statement? Write out two more relevant points.

b. Mia completely agrees with the statement about public libraries. Look at her list of ideas below.

☑ Reading for pleasure is a thing of the past and people now have better things to do with their time

☑ Many people don't find the time to go to libraries

Disagree   **Agree**

1   5   10

my view

☑ While libraries are meant to encourage all children to read, it is only parents who are keen on reading that take their children. They would have their own books at home anyway.

☑ The opening hours of libraries do not fit in when most people are free to go there

c. Can you identify two ideas that are very similar? Identify one point that is not needed, or combine the ideas.

d. Add two further points that agree with the statement. Check back against the key words of the statement to make sure that they support it.

Exam tip ✔

Beware of using the same idea or point more than once. Your argument should present and explore one idea or point per paragraph. Each idea or point must be *different* to support your view.

Vocabulary choices

Activity 5

Read this part of a speech on libraries given by the author Philip Pullman. It is a powerful speech about the closure of the libraries in Oxfordshire, his home county. Before you consider your own and other students' answers, identify some of the features used by Pullman for effect.

- What reasons does he give for supporting libraries?
- What language devices does he use to strengthen his argument?
- Select three words or phrases that you think stand out as memorable in his piece.

Two examples have been done for you.

Leave the libraries alone. You don't understand their value.

Proper noun to convey facts

Rhetorical question – the author is talking directly to the reader

I still remember the first library ticket I ever had. It must have been about 1957. My mother took me to the public library just off Battersea Park Road and enrolled me. I was thrilled. All those books, and I was allowed to borrow whichever I wanted! And I remember some of the first books I borrowed and fell in love with: the Moomin books by Tove Jansson; a French novel for children called *A Hundred Million Francs*; why did I like that? Why did I read it over and over again, and borrow it many times? I don't know. But what a gift to give a child, this chance to discover that you can love a book and the characters in it, you can become their friend and share their adventures in your own imagination.

And the secrecy of it! The blessed privacy! No-one else can get in the way, no-one else can invade it, no-one else even knows what's going on in that wonderful space that opens up between the reader and the book. That open democratic[1] space full of thrills, full of excitement and fear, full of astonishment, where your own emotions and ideas are given back to you clarified[2], magnified, purified, valued. You're a citizen of that great democratic space that opens up between you and the book. And the body that gave it to you is the public library. Can I possibly convey the magnitude[3] of that gift?

[1]democratic – open to everyone

[2]clarified – made clear

[3]magnitude – great size

Activity 6

Now read the opening of an answer by one student on this topic.

They have used some interesting and relevant points and adopted a confident style of argument. However, there is some informality and repetition in the language.

Sometimes a word or phrase can be repeated for deliberate effect to emphasize a point. But sometimes, it can show a need to widen vocabulary.

a. Identify which words need changing in this answer to show off a wider vocabulary. Make suggestions for some more interesting and engaging words.

b. Identify any words or phrases that are informal or colloquial. Make suggestions for some more formal alternatives.

> 'Public libraries are a thing of the past. They are an unnecessary public expense in modern society.'

Harry

Nowadays if you asked most young people whether they have been to their local public library in the last six months, the answer would be 'no'. They wouldn't even be able to direct you to a library because they had never been to a library. They would say libraries are boring. They would say reading books is a pretty boring way of spending time. But the fact that lots of young people may give this opinion does not mean that it is right. And it certainly does not mean that funding of today's libraries should not continue. Instead it tells us that these young people need help to learn about the importance of libraries. Young people need educating about libraries. They have got it wrong.

Books, books, books! This is what libraries are about. However far we have come in our information gathering since the internet, there is nothing like picking up a real traditional book. Five years ago newspaper reports claimed that the publishing industry was going to go out of business because of electronic communication, but in fact now the sales of the Kindle are going down and books are coming back into fashion. It is pretty fashionable to be a reader. It is a way of educating yourself. Therefore libraries are a way of keeping a great and important tradition alive.

Structuring your writing

Once you have generated your points, you need to think about how to organize them into a complete piece of writing. Decide how you want to guide your reader through your ideas to reach your conclusion. You should consider:

● creating an engaging opening to draw your readers in

● grouping your ideas into paragraphs

● the best order for your points

● using a variety of structural features to build your ideas.

Here is an exam-style writing question:

'Reality TV shows are a negative influence on today's youth. They emphasize show and celebrity over hard work and real talent.'

Write a letter in response to a magazine article presenting this view, in which you present your personal opinion.

Activity 7

Look back at the plan you created in response to this writing task in Activity 3.

• Is there anything you want to add or change?

• Is each idea or point different or do some overlap?

• Have you dealt with every key aspect of the statement?

• Have you grouped all 'agree' points together and all 'disagree' points together?

• Have you selected the best four or five ideas to use in your plan?

Writing your introduction

Once you have planned the structure of your writing, you must write the introductory paragraph. This should:

● establish the topic you are considering

● set out your point of view in relation to the statement generally rather than giving specific points of argument

● engage your reader

● demonstrate awareness of the text type/form and purpose.

Activity 8

Two students have started to write their responses to the following task.

> 'The standard of manners in this country is awful. It is time parents and schools taught young people how to act with consideration and politeness.'
>
> Write an article for the local newspaper in which you either agree or disagree with this view.

Read the opening paragraphs of their articles below and decide whether you think each response will:

- agree with the statement
- disagree with the statement
- present a balanced viewpoint.

Jamie

Backchatting adults, no more thank yous and demanding more of the school. How many of us have noticed that things have changed in the behaviour of new pupils coming to our school? It was only last week that a lunchtime assistant was away after an incident where a Year 7 pupil was verbally abusive to her. In our recent survey in the sixth form, 85 percent of students were concerned about the behaviour of younger students around the school. Well I would certainly agree that manners in today's society are going downhill fast. Though it's not just schools and parents that can teach primary school children a thing or too, but those of us at secondary school as well. We must remember that to make blanket statements like this does not account for the many different young people from different home lives that make up our society.

Judith

There are many complaints about young people today. Criticism of the next generation is almost a fashion and maybe this has always been the case. It was only last week that I read an article about how, as a result of computer games, and orders to Siri on their iphones, that young people have now forgotten how to be polite. It claimed that instead of using polite language, they are ordering adults around without a please or thank you. Yet, the young people that I mix with on a daily basis, are not bad- mannered at all. Things may be different in the twenty-first century and life may be less formal, but we definitely know how to behave politely in situations where we need to. This article will explore how many of us have much better manners than the adults who brought us up.

Exam tip ✔

If you see a good phrase in a piece of writing, store it up to help improve your own writing!

Exam tip ✔

Each point or idea in your plan should provide you with a paragraph of writing. It is essential that you organize your writing into paragraphs to meet the key skills required for AO5 in writing.

One of the key things your introductory paragraph needs to do is engage your reader. Look at the following list of techniques you could use to do this.

Key term

anecdote: a brief personal story, often used to add personal interest or to emphasize the writer's experience of the topic

Technique	Example
A rhetorical question	How many of us have noticed that things have changed in the behaviour of new pupils coming to our school?
A list	… spitting, burping and leaving a mess.
A short sentence	Things certainly need to change.
An assertion	Today's young people have lost knowledge about good manners.
An interesting or shocking fact	85 percent of students were concerned about the behaviour of younger students around the school.
An explanation of purpose	This article will explore how many of us have much better manners than the adults who have brought us up.
A balanced statement	Things may be different in the 21st century and life may be less formal, but we definitely know how to behave politely in situations where we need to.
An **anecdote**	It was only last week that…

Activity 9

Remind yourself of the following exam-style writing task:

> 'Reality TV shows are a negative influence on today's youth. They emphasize show and celebrity over hard work and real talent.'
>
> Write a letter in response to a magazine article presenting this view, in which you present your opinion.

a. List the techniques from the table above that you would use in the introductory paragraph of a letter to a parenting magazine. For each technique, explain why you have chosen it.

b. Now write the opening of your letter.

Key terms

sign off: to end a letter using a phrase such as 'Yours sincerely'

salutation: greeting in a letter such as 'Dear…'

Exam tip ✔ SPAG

If you are asked to write a formal letter in the exam, remember to set out your letter in the correct format. If you know the name of the person you are writing to, **sign off** 'Yours sincerely'. If you don't know the name of the person you could use the **salutation** 'Dear Sir or Madam' and sign off 'Yours faithfully'.

Learn how to spell:

faithfully

sincerely

Writing your response

When writing in the exam it is important to use your plan to make sure that each idea is clearly presented and developed.

- Check that each point made at the beginning of a paragraph is developed and supported by what follows.
- Avoid writing a one-sentence paragraph, unless you are consciously using this structural feature for emphasis.

Look at the exam-style writing task below:

> 'A vegetarian diet is the only humane and healthy diet. We should all follow this because eating meat is murder.'
>
> Write a speech in which you either agree or disagree with this view.

One student, Finn has listed the following three ideas he wants to include in his speech:

Finn

- Too much processed meat has been proven to lead to cancer.
- It is hypocritical to be an animal lover who keeps pets and at the same time eats animals.
- There are many excellent vegetarian restaurants and recipe books now compared to ten years ago.

Now look at how one of the points has been developed into a paragraph.

> How many of you here today eat meat, regularly? How many of you have a ham sandwich in your school packed lunch today? Well, it is definitely the case that a heavily meat-based diet is an unhealthy one. Too much processed meat such as ham and sausages has been proved to lead to illnesses such as bowel cancer. It would be a high price to pay just for the pleasure of taste, to have your life shortened because of eating too much meat. So it is true to say that a vegetarian diet is generally more healthy, though a balanced diet with some meat is also fine in terms of personal health in my opinion.

Activity 10

Look back at the student's response above and note down any phrases that identify this text as a speech. Remember to make the text type of your writing clear.

Creating cohesion

To achieve your target grade for the Writing section in Paper 2, you must connect your ideas together and develop your points. Writing paragraphs using discourse markers creates coherence in your work. You should not write your points as disconnected paragraphs or as a list.

Examples of discourse markers might include 'on the other hand', 'therefore', 'in the same way', 'in contrast'.

The following structures are ways to present your viewpoint and link ideas together to present a smooth, organized argument to the reader. Notice how they always end with emphasis on the point of view you are arguing.

1. **Problem plus solution:** Outline a problem and give a solution – the solution should be in line with the point of view you are arguing.

2. **Cause and effect:** Explain the negative or positive effects of a particular cause to support the point of view you are arguing.

3. **Argument plus counter argument:** Outline an argument that others might put forward on the topic, then dismiss that point of view with your own viewpoint.

Activity 11

Look at the following paragraphs that two students have written in response to the writing task about manners in Activity 8.

a. For each paragraph, identify the structure it uses (Problem plus solution/Cause and effect/Argument plus counter argument).

b. List any key words in the student response that helped you to make your decision. Include some useful discourse markers that are used to create cohesion.

Corey

One negative effect of children being constantly plugged in to parents' phones and tablets from an early age, just to keep them quiet, is that they have learnt to bark orders at inanimate objects. Not only that, they have heard their parents ordering Siri to 'tell me the nearest coffee shop' with not so much as a please or thank you. It is no wonder then that the nicer elements of conversation and manners have been lost.

Hannah

It is parents themselves who have contributed to the bad manners of the next generation. It is parents who have given up on insisting on please and thank you. It is them who have allowed their children to sit in front of the TV when they eat their tea rather than engaging them in social skills and polite conversation. Or so we are told by head teachers. But without the school's support, what use is it to insist on please and thank you at home? When parents stagger in from a long day at work, earning money to keep their children topped up with school shoes, sports equipment and bus fare for school, they are shattered. Who can blame them for heading to the comfort of the sofa with their kids and enjoying tea there together?

Try it yourself

Remind yourself of the following exam-style writing task:

> 'Reality TV shows are a negative influence on today's youth. They emphasize show and celebrity over hard work and real talent.'
>
> Write a letter in response to a magazine article presenting this view in which you present your opinion.

Exam tip ✔

Learn this list of discourse markers to prepare for your exam.

Activity 12

a. Look back at your plan for this example question and the introductory paragraph you have created so far.

b. Now continue writing your letter and complete your response on blank paper. Try to use some of the following discourse markers to connect your ideas and create coherent paragraphs.

Building your argument	Contrasting viewpoints	Asserting your point of view
it is not only the case	while some might say… others maintain	it is my view that
as a result	alternatively	it is undeniable that
therefore	however	it is a well-known fact that
in relation to this	nonetheless	it is clear to me that
as a result,	despite this	it is generally agreed that
not only… but also	on the other hand	
first… secondly… thirdly… finally	conversely	
in addition	in contrast	
another point	unlike this	
furthermore		
next		
similarly		

Language, tone and style

When writing a formal response in the exam, you must convey a clear tone and personal voice. Will your article add a little spark of humour? Will you adopt an angry, sad or sarcastic tone? Or will you adopt a serious, informed voice?

Read the letter below, published in a newspaper. It is written from a mother to her adult daughter and is part of a regular feature where readers write anonymously to share something they want to say to someone but cannot say in person. She expresses her views about how she feels about her daughter's choice not to eat meat or any animal products.

As you read, consider the language, tone and style that the mother has chosen in this article to describe how she feels about her daughter's views and behaviour.

A letter to... my daughter who hates me for not being vegan

When you told me you had decided to become a vegan[1], I was worried. You had always been a fussy eater and I feared that, with such a limited diet, you wouldn't get the
5 nutrition you needed.

But you were over 18, so it was your choice. In addition, you did begin to eat more fruit and vegetables and tried to include the right food and supplements in your diet, so I was at least
10 partly appeased[2].

You said your motivation was animal welfare and the environmental damage that was caused by agriculture. Fair enough.

With a younger child and a full-time job, I
15 found it a challenge to research and cook meals for you, but I took it on board. And when you left home for university, I made sure the car was packed with homemade vegan soup for your freezer.

But it is not enough for you that I accommodate   20
your choice. As you have explained many times, for you, veganism is not just about what you eat – it's a lifestyle. You have watched all the pro-vegan documentaries, read mountains of information on the internet and   25
can effortlessly reel off the soundbites. You have become passionate about the cause to the point of dogma[3]. You will not tolerate any opposing view. Crucially, you can no longer respect anyone who is not persuaded to go   30
vegan. And that means me.

I am open to at least some of your arguments and have made changes to my diet on account of information you have passed on to me

35 about farmed animals. But, as a middle-aged woman, my choices in life are narrowing and will continue to narrow. I have no intention of limiting those choices further by going vegan. In your eyes, that just makes me selfish.

40 When we meet, I take you to vegan restaurants and embrace the choices available. I send you vegan recipes and seek out vegan chocolate for you in the supermarket. I know that you appreciate my

45 efforts, but I also know that I will always fall short. I have stopped even trying to explain my reasons for not going vegan as it just ends up with both of us getting upset.

There is an uncomfortable contradiction for

50 me in all of this – I have brought you up to be a strong, powerful, compassionate young woman. I would expect you to be passionate about what you believe in. I have taught you that tolerance is vital, but that there is

55 a point when a line is crossed and certain behaviour cannot be tolerated. So I really can understand, in part, your attitude.

But I can't tell you how hard it is to live with the knowledge that my own daughter is sickened by me. It is so important to me to 60 feel worthy of your respect.

I hope that in time and with maturity, dogma may give way to a more open attitude. But my fear is that, while you may mellow in how outspoken you are about veganism, your 65 revulsion of me will remain vivid. And I will just have to live with that.

Anonymous

¹vegan – a person who does not eat any food that has animal origin, for example, meat, milk, cheese and butter

²appeased – satisfied

³dogma – a set of principles which are presented as absolutely true

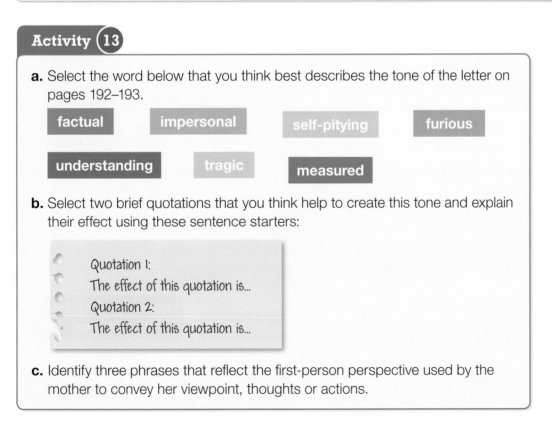

Activity 13

a. Select the word below that you think best describes the tone of the letter on pages 192–193.

| factual | impersonal | self-pitying | furious |

| understanding | tragic | measured |

b. Select two brief quotations that you think help to create this tone and explain their effect using these sentence starters:

> Quotation 1:
> The effect of this quotation is...
> Quotation 2:
> The effect of this quotation is...

c. Identify three phrases that reflect the first-person perspective used by the mother to convey her viewpoint, thoughts or actions.

Look again at a section of the letter below and consider the annotations that identify the language features the mother has used to create a skilful and engaging argument.

Conjunction to emphasize two opposing viewpoints

Repetition of first- and second-person pronouns to focus on the mother-daughter relationship

Media term to suggest the daughter has been influenced by the media. Critical tone

Discourse marker to emphasize an important point

But it is not enough for you that I accommodate your choice. As you have explained many times, for you, veganism is not just about what you eat – it's a lifestyle. You have watched all the pro-vegan documentaries, read mountains of information on the internet and can effortlessly reel off the soundbites. You have become passionate about the cause to the point of dogma. You will not tolerate any opposing view. Crucially, you can no longer respect anyone who is not persuaded to go vegan. And that means me.

Set of three to suggest the daughter's excessive activity

Ambitious vocabulary used accurately

Short sentence to emphasize finality and emotional upset

Activity 14

Now re-read the whole letter on pages 192–193 and identify some of the following structural and language features. Think about how the writer uses these features to:

- convey her viewpoint
- structure her writing
- explain her reasons
- convey her emotions.

Think about how you could use these features in your own writing.

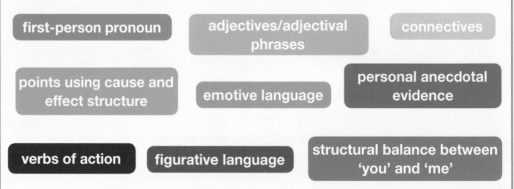

first-person pronoun

adjectives/adjectival phrases

connectives

points using cause and effect structure

emotive language

personal anecdotal evidence

verbs of action

figurative language

structural balance between 'you' and 'me'

Activity 15

Remind yourself of the following exam-style writing task:

'For today's busy families, finding time to schedule exercise for children is a luxury not a necessity. Schools should take responsibility for this, not parents.'

Write a letter to the local MP who made this statement, in which you explain your response to her opinion.

Read the introductory paragraph below and continue the letter, using what you have learned in the chapter so far.

Think about planning your points, structuring your writing and using carefully chosen vocabulary and discourse markers. Remember to lay out your letter correctly with the salutation and sign off.

Dear Ms Garner,

I am writing in response to your comments at the local meeting at Groveland sports centre last week suggesting that today's families have neither the time nor the responsibility for the exercise of their children...

Technical accuracy

In Section B of Paper 2, there are 16 marks available for AO6 (technical accuracy). To make sure that you gain as many marks for AO6 as possible, make sure that you:

- re-read your writing as you go and leave enough time for a final proofread at the end
- use a wide range of punctuation accurately
- use a range of ambitious vocabulary
- use a range of sentence forms for effect.

Using a range of sentence forms

To achieve your target grade, you need to demonstrate that you can use a variety of sentence forms. Beware of writing sentences that are all of similar length and a similar structure.

Remind yourself of the final sentences of the mother's letter on pages 192–193:

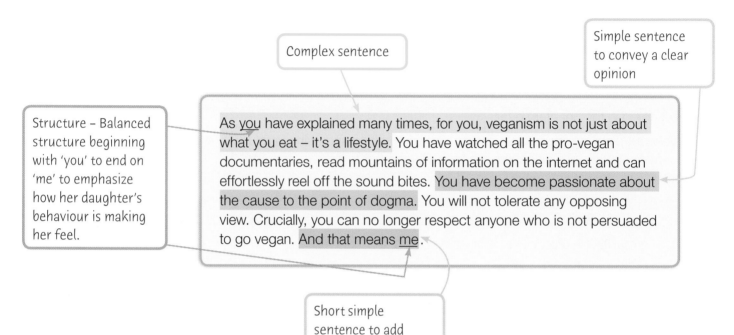

Complex sentence

Simple sentence to convey a clear opinion

Structure – Balanced structure beginning with 'you' to end on 'me' to emphasize how her daughter's behaviour is making her feel.

As you have explained many times, for you, veganism is not just about what you eat – it's a lifestyle. You have watched all the pro-vegan documentaries, read mountains of information on the internet and can effortlessly reel off the sound bites. You have become passionate about the cause to the point of dogma. You will not tolerate any opposing view. Crucially, you can no longer respect anyone who is not persuaded to go vegan. And that means me.

Short simple sentence to add impact and emotion.

Notice the variety of sentence forms used. The writer uses short sentences for emphasis, and a longer sentence with a sub-clause to reflect what she sees as her daughter's complex behaviour.

Activity 16

Now look back at the letter you completed in Activity 15.

a. Read through each paragraph carefully, looking for opportunities to include ambitious vocabulary, a range of linguistic devices and a variety of sentence forms to create deliberate effects.

b. Rewrite any paragraphs that you think could be improved.

Using a range of punctuation

You also need to show that you can use a range of punctuation successfully in your writing. Remind yourself of the purpose and use of punctuation marks that might end or join sentences:

Punctuation mark	Purpose and use	Example
Question mark ?	This could be used to ask a rhetorical question of the reader.	For example, 'Where is the sense in young people experiencing public shame just for a desperate moment of fame?'
Exclamation mark !	This could be used to emphasize how ridiculous an opposing viewpoint is to you.	For example, 'Some people even believe that without training and hard work, a career in music is a real possibility!'
Ellipses …	This could be used to leave the reader thinking.	For example, 'An overnight blind date with a total stranger. A death run on skis that has actually killed contestants. What reality show writers will think of next we can only imagine…'
Colon :	This could be used to begin a list.	For example, 'The extremes TV stations go to to gain an audience continue to increase: a marriage to a stranger, detoxing on live TV or even eating live maggots.'
Semicolon ;	This should be used to link two closely connected sentences.	For example, 'There seem to be no limits to what people are prepared to do; we have seen so-called celebrities being unfaithful to their husbands as if they had forgotten they were on live TV.'

Activity 17

Look back again at the letter you completed in Activity 15.

a. Could you replace full stops with any of the above punctuation marks?

b. Edit your letter to make sure that you have used a range of punctuation successfully. You may need to redraft some of your sentences to enable you to do this.

Exam tip ✔

Avoid overusing certain types of punctuation.

For example, do not have a paragraph where every sentence ends with an exclamation mark or a piece of writing that is littered with questions.

Activity 18

Now that you have practised your writing skills, it's time to write a complete response to an exam-style Paper 2 Section B: Writing task.

> 'There have been too many accidents on adventurous residential activities run by schools for students. Extreme sports, dangerous experiences or adventures in developing countries are not appropriate for school trips.'
>
> Write an article for the travel section of a broadsheet newspaper in which you explain your point of view on adventurous school trips.

Remember to use your time carefully, dividing it between planning, writing and proofreading your work. For example:

- planning (5–10 minutes)
- writing (30–35 minutes)
- checking, proofreading and making final improvements (5 minutes).

Progress check

Now that you have practised the skills needed for the Writing task, carry out the progress check below.

a. Use several highlighter pens of different colours to highlight passages of your answer in Activity 18 to show where you have satisfied each of the key skills below.

Key Skills I can:	Confident I can do this.	OK Sometimes I can do this.	Not sure I need to practise this more.
match the register I use in my writing to the audience I am writing for			
ensure my writing is consistently matched to purpose			
choose vocabulary for effect and use a range of linguistic devices to achieve effects			
ensure my writing is engaging, with a range of connected ideas			
use clear paragraphs and link them using discourse markers			
use a variety of structural features effectively			
write in full and accurate sentences			
use a range of punctuation			
use a variety of sentence forms in my writing to achieve specific effects on the reader			
control my use of Standard English and grammar			
spell correctly, including complex and irregular words			
use a range of vocabulary, including some sophisticated words.			

b. If your answer is missing any of these skills, or you think it could be stronger, go back and improve your answer. You could work with a partner to offer each other feedback on your responses.

Sample Exam Paper 1

Source A

This extract is the first half of a short story, 'Reunion', by John Cheever, first published in 1962. The story is set in the United States and describes the meeting of a young man called Charlie with his father. Charlie has not had contact with his father for a long time.

Extract from 'Reunion' by John Cheever

The last time I saw my father was in Grand Central Station[1]. I was going from my grandmother's in the Adirondacks[2] to a cottage on the Cape[3] that my mother had rented, and I wrote my father that I would be in New York between trains for an hour and a half and asked if we could have lunch together. His secretary wrote to say that he would meet me at the information booth at

5   noon, and at twelve o'clock sharp I saw him coming through the crowd. He was a stranger to me — my mother divorced him three years ago, and I hadn't been with him since — but as soon as I saw him I felt that he was my father, my flesh and blood, my future and my doom. I knew that when I was grown I would be something like him; I would have to plan my campaigns within his limitations. He was a big, good-looking man, and I was terribly happy to see him again. He

10   struck me on the back and shook my hand. 'Hi, Charlie,' he said. 'Hi, boy. I'd like to take you up to my club, but it's in the Sixties[4], and if you have to catch an early train I guess we'd better get something to eat around here.' He put his arm around me, and I smelled my father the way my mother sniffs a rose. It was a rich compound of whiskey, after-shave lotion, shoe polish, woollens, and the rankness of a mature male. I hoped that someone would see us together. I wished that we

15   could be photographed. I wanted some record of our having been together.

We went out of the station and up a side street to a restaurant. It was still early, and the place was empty. The bartender was quarrelling with a delivery boy, and there was one very old waiter in a red coat down by the kitchen floor. We sat down, and my father hailed the waiter in a loud voice. '*Kellner*[5]!' he shouted. '*Garçon*[6]! *Cameriere*[7]! *You!*' His boisterousness in the empty restaurant seemed out of

20   place. 'Could we have a little service here?' he shouted. 'Chop-chop.' Then he clapped his hands. This caught the waiter's attention, and he shuffled over to our table.

'Were you clapping your hands at me?' he asked.

'Calm down, calm down, *sommelier*[8],' my father said. 'If it isn't too much to ask of you — if it wouldn't be too much above and beyond the call of duty, we would like a couple of Beefeater

25   Gibsons[9].'

'I don't like to be clapped at,' the waiter said.

'I should have brought my whistle,' my father said. 'I have a whistle that is audible only to the ears of old waiters. Now, take out your little pad and your little pencil and see if you can get this straight: two Beefeater Gibsons. Repeat after me: two Beefeater Gibsons.'

30 'I think you'd better go somewhere else,' the waiter said quietly.

'That,' said my father, 'is one of the most brilliant suggestions I have ever heard. Come on, Charlie, let's get the hell out of here.'

I followed my father out of that restaurant into another. He was not so boisterous this time. Our drinks came, and he cross-questioned me about the baseball season. He then struck the edge of
35 his empty glass with his knife and began shouting again. '*Garçon! Kellner! You!* Could we trouble you to bring us two more of the same.'

'How old is the boy?' The waiter asked.

'That, my father said, is none of your goddamned business.'

'I'm sorry, sir,' the waiter said, 'but I won't serve the boy another drink.'

40 'Well, I have some news for you,' my father said. 'I have some very interesting news for you. This doesn't happen to be the only restaurant in New York. They've opened another on the corner. Come on, Charlie.'

He paid the bill, and I followed him out of that restaurant into another.

[1]Grand Central – the busiest railway station in New York City
[2]Adirondacks
[3]The Cape] – places in America
[4]the Sixties – an area of streets in New York
[5]Kellner – German for 'waiter'

[6]Garçon – French for waiter
[7]Cameriere – Italian for waiter
[8]Sommelier – term used for a wine waiter (originally French)
[9]Beefeater Gibsons – a cocktail

Section A: Reading

Answer **all** questions in this section.

You are advised to spend about 45 minutes on this section.

| 0 | 1 | Read again the first paragraph of the Source from **lines 1 to 5**.

List **four** things from this part of the text about Charlie. **[4 marks]**

0 2   Look in detail at this extract from **lines 5 to 15** of the Source:

> He was a stranger to me — my mother divorced him three years ago, and I hadn't been
> with him since — but as soon as I saw him I felt that he was my father, my flesh and blood,
> my future and my doom. I knew that when I was grown I would be something like him; I
> would have to plan my campaigns within his limitations. He was a big, good-looking man,
> and I was terribly happy to see him again. He struck me on the back and shook my hand.
> 'Hi, Charlie,' he said. 'Hi, boy. I'd like to take you up to my club, but it's in the Sixties, and if
> you have to catch an early train I guess we'd better get something to eat around here.' He
> put his arm around me, and I smelled my father the way my mother sniffs a rose. It was a
> rich compound of whiskey, after-shave lotion, shoe polish, woollens, and the rankness of
> a mature male. I hoped that someone would see us together. I wished that we could be
> photographed. I wanted some record of our having been together.

How does the writer use language to describe Charlie's father?

You could include the writer's choice of:

- words and phrases
- language features and techniques
- sentence forms.   **[8 marks]**

0 3   You now need to think about the **whole** of the **Source**.

This text is the first half of a short story.

How has the writer structured the text to interest you as a reader?

You could write about:

- what the writer focuses your attention on at the beginning
- how and why the writer changes this focus as the Source develops
- any other structural features that interest you.   **[8 marks]**

0 4   Focus this part of your answer on the second part of the Source, from **line 22 to the end.**

A student, having read this section of the text said: 'This part of the text emphasizes the
contrast between Charlie's hopes about meeting his father and the reality of the experience.
You get a sense of his increasing disappointment.'

To what extent do you agree?

In your response, you could:

- write about your own impressions of Charlie and the situation he finds himself in
- evaluate how the writer has created these impressions
- support your opinions with references to the text.   **[20 marks]**

Section B: Writing

You are advised to spend about 45 minutes on this section.

Write in full sentences.

You are reminded of the need to plan your answer.

You should leave enough time to check your work at the end.

0 5 You have been asked to contribute to a new travel magazine for young people.

Either: Write a description suggested by this picture.

Or: Write the opening part of a story in which your main character experiences disappointment.

(24 marks for content and organization

16 marks for technical accuracy)

[40 marks]

Sample Exam Paper 2

Source A

Sad Eyes Empty Lives by The Captive Animals Protection Society

There are over 400 zoos in the UK today, ranging from small farm parks and butterfly zoos to large safari parks and aquaria. Worldwide there are probably more than 10,000 zoos, with hundreds of thousands of animals held captive. Zoos are a relic of a bygone[1] age – a Victorian concept which, as our knowledge of the animal kingdom grows, becomes even less palatable. An increasing
5   number of people are concerned about keeping wild animals captive. So zoos claim they are on a greater mission than simple entertainment: for conservation, education and research. Zoos now favour terms like 'wildlife park' or even 'sanctuary'. The Captive Animals' Protection Society is totally opposed to the incarceration[2] of animals and believes that zoos misinform rather than educate, and further, divert funds from positive conservation. Animals remain threatened or are
10   even driven to extinction, whilst precious resources are drained away on expensive, high-profile breeding projects with no serious hope of success.

In the wild, animals react to their surroundings, avoiding predators, seeking food and interacting with others of their species doing what they have evolved for. Consequently, even what might seem 'larger' or 'better' enclosures may be completely impoverished in terms of the animals' real needs.
15   Frustration and boredom are commonplace amongst animals in zoos and can lead to obsessive behaviours in the form of pacing, swaying, and even self-mutilation. This is known as stereotypic behaviour and such pointless, repetitive movements have also been noted in people with mental illnesses. With nothing to do, animals in zoos go out of their minds. Studies have found that lions in zoos spend 48% of their time pacing and 40% of elephants performed stereotypic behaviours.

20   Even diets are unnatural. Zebras in zoos become overweight as the grass they are given is higher in calories than the grasses of the African savannah. The resulting obesity can affect fertility as well as make the animal susceptible to nutritional illness. CAPS have filmed adult gorillas in zoos repeatedly eating their own vomit. A gorilla biologist told CAPS: 'I have never seen wild gorillas perform R&R (regurgitate and re-ingest, as it's known in the zoo world, being such a well known
25   byproduct of captivity) and I have never spoken to anyone who has. In fact, I have never seen a wild gorilla vomit.' Some animals suffer such serious behavioural problems in zoos that they are given anti-depressants, tranquillisers and anti-psychotic drugs to control their behaviours. Zoos often refer to the animals they confine as being 'ambassadors' of their species, but just what message does it give when we see animals in such unnatural conditions, displaying disturbed
30   behaviours? […]

Education

Zoos claim that seeing a live wild animal gives an unparalleled appreciation of the power and wonder of nature, but what are they really showing us? 'Most visits to most zoos throughout

35 history have served only as diversions for the curious. Most zoo animals have traditionally been reduced to caricatures of their wild cousins.' (Zoo director David Hancocks)

We don't need to be wealthy to see animals in the wild. Wildlife is all around us, whether we live in a city or the countryside. From birds in the garden to badgers and deer in the woodland, we can all explore wildlife in its natural habitat with as little – or as much – effort as we want to put in. […]

Zoos claim that they afford people the opportunity to see something that many will never see in the wild.
40 This is true; we will have to make do with books, magazines and television. However, can a few minutes of entertainment ever justify the tragedy of the disturbed behaviours and suffering we have outlined?

¹bygone – past   ²incarceration – imprisonment

Source B

Read the two diary extracts by Anne Chalmers, the daughter of a university professor. She writes about her family trip from Scotland to England in 1830 and the social events she takes part in while staying in London and Bridport. This includes a visit to Regent's Park Zoo in London which was only opened that year and was the first of its kind in England.

A visit to England by Anne Chalmers

Saturday, 22nd May

Mrs. J. Parker and Mr. Duncan came to breakfast. Mrs. Upchar and her daughters visited us early, lest we should have gone out before they came. I think Mrs. Upchar the most lady-like person I have seen since I left home. We walked to the Zoological Garden in Regent's Park. It is a most delightful spectacle, the animals have so much more liberty than in common menageries¹. The
5 enclosures are large, and all except the wild animals are kept in the open air during the daytime. The tiger seemed to feel annoyed at being looked on in what it esteemed a state of degradation, and walked up and down its narrow prison as if it would fain increase its boundaries, and the lion lay asleep – perhaps dreaming of its own native forests, or of a delicious banquet which it tasted only *once*, but remembers with continued zest, consisting of a young child which had been brought to it
10 by its mother. Many more animals and birds were there than I can enumerate, but I shall mention the monkeys, whose tricks were very diverting. I brought them some nuts and biscuits, and whenever they saw them there was a commotion in their cages, and paws were stretched out in all directions for them. While I was bending to give a weak one a nut, which a superior was taking from it, my bonnet was seized from a cage above and the front nearly torn from it. The keeper let them out from
15 their confinement into large arbours in the open air, where were hung swings and ropes, and certainly the gymnastics of the Greenwich boys were far exceeded by these agile creatures. They flung themselves from rope to rope and to the side of the cage with immense celerity. Next in agility to the

monkeys were the bears, though in a more clumsy style. They begged for buns, and clambered up a long pole to amuse the bystanders, who rewarded them with cakes.

20   On leaving the Garden we met Sir James Mackintosh on horseback. He looks very graceful. I suppose he feels his wife's death, of which he heard the very day we were with him. We met a little gig in which we drove home the rest of the way. Among the calling cards we found Mr. Spencer Percival's, whom I was very sorry to have missed. Lady and Miss Butler called. Miss B. proposed walking in Regent's Park with me some evening.

25   Thursday, 10th June

We went into Bridport and first called at Dr. Roberts', the apothecary's[2], and saw his curiosities. I never saw such a melange of things: cases of stuffed birds, lions' skins, leopards, Indian gods, models of churches, antiquities, fantastic-looking machinery (made by Dr. R. himself, who seems quite a virtuoso), a large case filled with stones, and here and there bits of glass twirling round meant to represent a
30   waterfall, a clock in which a bird sings a German air, moving its beak with great execution, etc. There we were introduced to two ladies, who followed Papa the whole day after, and, having discovered he was to be at Mr. Foster's at tea, went without invitation there. After leaving Dr. Roberts, Papa, Mamma, and my Uncle left Mrs. Chalmers and I, and we went to several shops and I was introduced to some of the shopkeepers, particularly one, a Mr. Stephens, from whom we bought some articles…

[1]menageries – travelling show displays of exotic animals popular before zoos were introduced   [2]apothecary – a herbalist or traditional pharmacist

Section A: Reading

Answer **all** questions in this section.

You are advised to spend about 45 minutes on this section.

0 1   Read again the first part of Source A from **lines 1 to 19**.

Choose **four** statements below which are TRUE.

- Shade the boxes of the ones that you think are true.
- Choose a maximum of four statements.

A   Zoos are a Victorian idea.

B   Modern zoos are often naming themselves wildlife parks or sanctuaries.

C   The writer believes zoos are important for animal research.

D   The writer believes zoos are a waste of money.

E   Obsessive behaviour can be seen in some wild animals that are kept in zoos. ⬭

F   Zoo enclosures allow animals to behave as they would in the wild. ⬭

G   Elephants are the most endangered species kept in zoos. ⬭

H   Zoos are preventing animal mutilation. ⬭

[4 marks]

0 2   You need to refer to **Source A** and **Source B** for this question.

Use details from **both** Sources. Write a summary of the different ways animal behaviour is described by the writers. **[8 marks]**

0 3   You now need to refer **only** to **Source A**, from **line 31 to the end**.

How does the writer from CAPS (The Captive Animals Protection Society) use language to criticize zoos' claims for being educational? **[12 marks]**

0 4   For this question, you need to refer to the **whole of Source A** together with the **whole of Source B**.

Compare how the two writers convey their different views and experiences of animals.

In your answer, you could:

- compare their views and experiences

- compare the methods they use to convey those views and experiences

- support your ideas with references to both texts. **[16 marks]**

Section B: Writing

You are advised to spend about 45 minutes on this section.

Write in full sentences.

You are reminded of the need to plan your answer.

You should leave enough time to check your work at the end.

0 5   'Social media is just like a zoo. The only difference is that people come to stare and poke fun at each other, not animals.'

Write an article for a broadsheet newspaper in which you explain your point of view on this statement.

(24 marks for content and organization

16 marks for technical accuracy)

[40 marks]

Glossary

actions: the things someone does

adjectival phrase: a group of words that explain a noun or pronoun; it can come before or after the noun/pronoun

adjective: a word that describes something named by a noun or pronoun

anecdote: a brief personal story, often used to add personal interest or to emphasize the writer's experience of the topic

assertion: a confident and forceful statement of fact or belief that is presented without supporting evidence

chronologically: organized in time order

coherence and cohesion: the way a piece of writing links together in terms of vocabulary, phrases, clauses, sentences and paragraphs

consistently: throughout, constantly

contrast: strong difference

critically: giving evidence-based reasons for your judgements. It does not mean to 'criticize' the writer.

dialogue: direct speech

discourse marker: words used to direct a reader through a text

evaluating: forming an idea about something in order to explain and interpret it

evaluate: to assess something and understand its quality

explicit: clearly stated; you just need to find it

implicit: suggested; you have to interpret the text to work it out for yourself

infer: work out meaning from what someone implies rather than from an explicit statement

inference: an opinion drawn from what someone implies, rather than from an explicit statement

interpret: explain the meaning of something in your own words, showing your understanding

irony: the technique of using words to convey a meaning that is the opposite of their literal meaning

metaphor: a comparison showing the similarity between two quite different things, where one is described as the other

obituary: a news article reporting the recent death of a person, usually includes details about their life and achievements

paraphrase: rewrite the meaning using your own words rather than the author's

personification: giving human qualities or emotions to something non-human

register: the kind of words (for example: formal, informal, literary) and the manner of writing

review: a text that gives opinion and information about a commodity such as a book, film or meal, and makes a judgement about it

salutation: greeting in a letter such as 'Dear...'

setting: the place or surroundings where an event takes place or something is positioned

sibilance: a literary device where repetition of 's' creates a hissing sound

sign off: to end a letter using a phrase such as 'Yours sincerely'

simile: a comparison showing the similarity between two quite different things, stating that one is like the other

structure: how a text is built and organized in sections

style: the language choices a writer makes

summarize: to give the main points of something briefly

synonym: a word with a similar meaning

synthesize: to combine information and ideas from different texts

theme: a central idea running through a text, often reflected by patterns of words that are linked to it, for example, love, violence, power

tone: a way of writing which conveys the writer's attitude towards either the reader or the subject matter

verbs: words that mark actions, events, processes and states. They usually have a tense, either present, past or future.

viewpoint: the opinion of the writer on the topic in question